P9-CRK-096

Customer Service

TRAINING

Includes CD-ROM with
Ready-to-Use Microsoft
PowerPoint™ Presentations

Exercises, Handouts, Assessments, and Tools
to Help You:

✔ Create Fantastic Customer Service to Meet Your
Specific Needs

✔ Raise the Bar for Service Excellence

✔ Become a More Effective and Efficient Facilitator

✔ Ensure Training Is on Target and Gets Results

ASTD

Linking People,
Learning & Performance

Maxine Kamin

Ordering Information: Books published by ASTD can be ordered by calling 800.628.2783 or 703.683.8100, or via the Website at www.astd.org.

Library of Congress Catalog Card Number: 2002104902

ISBN: 1-56286-330-4

The ASTD Trainer's WorkShop Series

The ASTD Trainer's WorkShop Series is designed to be a practical, hands-on road map to help you quickly develop training in key business areas. Each book in the series offers all the exercises, handouts, assessments, structured experiences, and ready-to-use presentations needed to develop effective training sessions. In addition to easy-to-use icons, each book in the series includes a companion CD-ROM with PowerPoint presentations and electronic copies of all supporting material featured in the book.

Other books in the Trainer's WorkShop Series:

New Supervisor Training
John E. Jones and Chris W. Chen

New Employee Orientation
Karen Lawson

Contents

◆

Customer service is very personal. Our expectations vary according to circumstances and our own ideas about good service, but we all know really good customer service when we see it. It's that special touch that makes us feel like someone cares. It's a smile or a follow-up call. It's someone doing something memorable that we didn't expect.

As a training professional, you have great influence in facilitating memorable moments for external as well as internal customers. If you have purchased this book, you are already thinking about how you can become more of a strategic partner, working with leaders to create an environment that is rewarding for individuals at all levels of your organization and that has a positive impact on the bottom line. Congratulations on taking the initiative to learn more about providing excellent service and how you can initiate the change process.

It is my hope that this book will make your learning journey easier and provide you with practical exercises, activities, and plans you can use to create training that has a visible impact. *Customer Service Training* is about facilitating what every organization wants: fantastic service every time. You can be instrumental in creating a framework to improve significantly how internal service providers assist each other and, ultimately, deliver great service to customers.

The learning tools in this book were created with years of customer service research as a foundation for program development. There are certain behaviors and actions that theorists have determined are important for customers to be satisfied, and ways that have been discovered to build relationships that go beyond mere satisfaction to real customer loyalty and appreciation. In the last 20-plus years, the learning tools in this book have been used in *Fortune* 500 companies, small companies, city and county governments and agencies, universities, community colleges, schools, nonprofit organizations, airports, and entertainment enterprises. Training designs have been used with all levels of personnel, from executives to maintenance staff. With customized approaches for different groups, organizations have succeeded in implementing what it takes to deliver fantastic service.

New technology has allowed us to augment your training tools. This book comes complete with a CD that has PowerPoint slides, handouts, and exercises to print and copy. You're on your way with a click of the mouse.

In any human relations training program, there are tried-and-true concepts and exercises that have become part of an experienced trainer's vocabulary. Thanks go to all those who have passed these traditions on and who have made it possible to pass them on again to you.

Special thanks go to the following people: Dr. John E. Jones, one of the nation's leading training consultants, for allowing me to use the "Jones Window" exercise in chapter 14; to John Goodman, president of Technical Assistance Research Programs (TARP), for his untiring emailing and faxing of customer service statistics; and to Nancy Rehbine, for her lively Superhero exercise.

On a more personal note, my sincere gratitude goes to Dr. Brad Stocker, longtime friend and colleague, who took the time to review this document as only a true educator could do, while providing support and encouragement "over and above the call of duty." I am grateful also to Ingrid Levy Abrahams, another friend and colleague, who was instrumental in providing suggestions from an expert trainer's point of view, and to Karen Campbell, who assisted with the preparation of slides.

What would a preface be without kudos to the parents? I am eternally grateful to my terrific dad, Jack, an eloquent writer, mentor, and always an inspiration, and to my perfect mom, Enid, the consummate customer service provider who has devoted her talents to serving others, including providing unconditional support to me—the lucky daughter. To my awesome brother, Stan: your support was the topping on the cake.

Final thanks go to the incredibly personable and expert editors who worked on this book, Chris Cuomo and Christine Cotting, and to ASTD's Mark Morrow. These dedicated professionals really cared about preserving the content and intent of the training, and were just a joy and pleasure to get to know.

Have fun with your customer service training and with the customers who will receive and appreciate the benefits of your programs. I wish you great success in your quest to make a real difference and to achieve fantastic service every time.

Maxine Kamin
April 2002

Introduction:
Why Customer Service?

- ◆ Why customer service matters
- ◆ Some helpful statistics
- ◆ How training can help
- ◆ How to use this book and the CD

Excellent customer service is crucial for good business. This chapter discusses the importance of customer service and shows you how to use this workbook to develop an exciting customer service training program based on both theory and practice.

Why Customer Service Matters

Customer service—You can't live with it, and you can't live without it. With our rushed lifestyles, overloaded desktops, and fast-paced work schedules, we all are looking for a little comfort. Comfort might come in the form of someone waiting on us quickly and enthusiastically at a retail store. It might be found in a kind word when we are trying to get an insurance issue resolved, or a cheerful voice saying, "I'd be glad to get that for you," when you call Directory Assistance. The bottom line is that we want other people to be nice to us. It seems that being nice should not be that difficult. So why is it so rare?

That question baffles most consumers, and we all speculate about the answers. Even *Newsweek* has weighed in on the topic. In the article "Tired of Smile-Free Service?" Keith Naughton (2000) reports that employers are having difficulty finding good employees. When they do find them, it's not easy to keep them. To top it off, managers feel they have no control over workers who give poor service because they fear that pointing out deficiencies may cause employee turnover, and high turnover rates can be costly to an organization.

That is a sad state of affairs, but there is hope. Research tells us that turnover is higher in companies where employees have a poor view of customer service, and that employees are good predictors of customers' perceptions. It follows that increasing the quality of service can increase both customer loyalty

> Great service companies build a *humane* community (the organization and its partners) that *humanely* serves customers and the broader community in which they live.
>
> – Leonard Berry,
> *Discovering the Soul of Service*

and employee retention significantly. There are good people out there who would like to do good work. They may lack skills and so they appear unmotivated, or they may be job-hopping because they haven't found work environments that support their talents.

Training is a key element in improving quality. Good workers know that training is necessary for success on the job and for future career growth. With the proper training and support, and a service environment that is customer-focused and humane, employees will have the tools they need to give customers what they want and deserve: *fantastic service every time*.

How This Book Can Help

This workbook can help organizations identify the principles of good customer service and can help trainers develop programs that raise the bar regarding service excellence. By getting involved in work-related scenarios and discussions, participants will have the opportunity to reinforce skills they already have, to learn new skills, and to see customer service in a fresh light. Training is a good way to honor and reinforce the customer-focused work already happening in many organizations, and to motivate participants to discover the magic of fantastic customer service. When someone completes the sessions described in this workbook, he or she should have a renewed spirit for pleasing customers, and new tools for doing a better job.

The Value of Good Service

The U.S. Bureau of Labor Statistics (http://www.bls.gov/emp) predicts that for the years 2000–2010, service-producing industries will account for virtually all of the job growth in the United States. Service industries are growing at a fast pace internationally as well. It's a service world. Companies that will survive in the future are gearing up now to make customer service a priority. Good service is fundamental to success. With so much competition out there, companies cannot afford to ignore the importance of serving customers well.

The Internet also has influenced the role of service. With a click of a mouse, customers can buy anything from food to cars quickly and easily. They don't have to put up with the potential threat of rude service.

On the other hand, as John Naisbitt predicted in *Megatrends* (1982), the more high-tech we get, the more high touch we'll need. People need the personal, human touch in business dealings. They need human contact that is compassionate and kind, helpful and genuine. There is no substitute for caring. In customer service, that means caring about the whole customer experience. It includes determining whether the product does what the advertising says it is going to do, ensuring that deliveries are on time, providing relevant information, solving problems that arise, and following up as needed. Customer service is an art, not a science, but we can identify common elements that make the art form more effective. In the process, we also might make it more enjoyable for everyone involved.

Service is important to customers, and it is equally important for business growth. It is an essential—not a luxury to be practiced when there is time. Consider the following research findings compiled by the Forum Corporation (1988) on the basis of responses from more than 5,700 customers, employees, and managers. These statistics have stood the test of tme. New Forum research will be published in the near future.

- ◆ Customers are five times more likely to switch vendors because of perceived service problems than for price concerns or product quality issues.

- ◆ There is an inverse relationship between the elements of service quality that matter most to customers and those elements that companies perform best.

- ◆ The highest employee turnover rates are associated with those companies possessing the lowest service quality.

- ◆ The bottom line in customer service is that customers want to feel cared about and respected, and that they are more likely to return if these conditions are met.

- ◆ If customers' problems are resolved in a satisfactory manner, they are more likely to return to a business or organization and to be more loyal.

- ◆ If satisfied with service, an average customer's lifetime with an organization lasts approximately 10 years.

◆ Businesses that provide superior customer service can charge more, realize greater profits, and increase their market share by an average of 6 percent per year.

These are dramatic results. Think about it: Some customers are dissatisfied with their purchases or services and never complain, but they never return to that business. Those who do complain and don't get results are not likely to return either, although the organization may never know about it. Those who are treated with concern and respect become even more loyal and inevitably recommend that business to others.

> It pays to keep a customer:
>
> *Satisfied customers =*
> *Money spent =*
> *Successful businesses*

The dollar amount that loyalty produces is significant. In fact, in a study done by Technical Assistance Research Programs (TARP) for the U.S. Office of Consumer Affairs, a formula was produced to demonstrate how complaints can generate profits (1986). The study found that corporate complaint-handling departments have earned in excess of 100 percent return-on-investment in industries as diverse as banking, utilities, retail, and automotive services. That is not surprising when you consider how the advantages of keeping customers are determined. Consider these findings:

◆ The original TARP study found that it costs up to five or six times more to attract new customers than to keep loyal ones. New research by TARP's John Goodman (1999), shows that the ratio can range from 2:1 to 20:1.

◆ A dissatisfied customer will tell approximately 10 people about his or her experience. Approximately 13 percent of those individuals will tell up to 20 more people.

◆ Satisfied customers will tell between three and five people about a positive experience.

◆ Seventy percent of dissatisfied customers who do not get their complaints resolved to their satisfaction will not continue doing business with that organization.

CUSTOMER SERVICE IN GOVERNMENT AGENCIES

Customer service initiatives can be just as important for government organizations as they are for businesses, even though most government agencies are not for profit. Better service enhances productivity, and treating customers right the first time saves time and money. Creating satisfied customers reduces the likelihood that irate citizens will take their complaints to higher sources, or to a public forum where negative word-of-mouth can be damaging. In many contexts, government agencies have seen outsourcing and privatizing as solutions to poor customer service and inefficiency. But outsourcing has failed on many occasions. Customer service initiatives can improve government service as well as public perception of government agencies.

How Training Can Help
Frontline Staff and Management

This program is for all those frontline champions who struggle with customer service issues daily—for the battered and the bruised; for the silent heroes of the customer service movement who, for the most part, manage to survive. It is for people who need to detox a bit. With the help of a good facilitator they will learn that they are not alone and that help is on the way.

This program is also for new employees who have not yet been bombarded by the many challenges of customer service work. Training will give new employees the tools they will need to turn potentially difficult situations into successful interactions.

Although this workbook is not primarily designed for management personnel, these programs have been used with great success to show executives, managers, and supervisors what frontline staff will be learning in training sessions. Chapter 10 also includes specific activities and exercises that can be used to train management teams.

The Realities of Training

Some disappointing news is that not all participants will stand up and cheer about taking part in customer service training. Trainees may not greet you with glee—some will be seated with folded arms and pursed lips. You may wonder if your tires are going to be slashed. Some trainees don't want to be there because they already see themselves as customer service superstars. Some have been sent by their managers against their will.

Others will be glad that their colleagues are in the class, and they may even wish that their managers were there, too. Some will be happy to be included in a training session that will help them grow and that will teach them ways to give better service.

Customer Service Training is designed to include a lot of interaction, so that participants with a range of attitudes can get involved. It enables employees to discover what they think good customer service is, and what it is not. By drawing on what everyone knows about good customer service, the activities in the workbook encourage open communication.

How to Use This Workbook

You can use this book to prepare for your program in several ways. The following ready-made programs include full agendas and all the materials you need for thorough and effective customer service training:

- One-hour session (chapter 7)
- Half-day session (chapter 8)
- One-day program (chapter 9).

You also may use your own combination of activities to create different designs. Adjust the length of the programs and exercises as you see fit, depending on the duration and purpose of your training.

- Choose the learning activities in chapters 13 and 14 to fit your needs, and create your own design.
- Combine some of the learning activities in chapters 13 and 14 with your own exercises, activities, and lessons.

The learning activities in this workbook include suggested timeframes, but those are approximate guides. Times can vary, depending on the receptivity and active participation of the groups you are training, and your own agendas in training. A discussion of factors that might influence your decision to use a particular program is included in chapter 4.

What's in This Workbook and on the CD?

All of the training materials in this workbook also are included on the accompanying CD so that you can easily run PowerPoint presentations and print out and copy other materials. To get a sense of your many options, review the contents of the CD to see how they relate to the material in the printed book. Read the document *How to Use the Contents of the CD.txt* included on the CD and read the appendix, "Using the Compact Disc," at the end of the workbook. Below is an overview of the materials included in the workbook and on the CD.

LEARNING ACTIVITIES

The learning activities you will find in this workbook include the following:

- **Exercises.** Exercises are designed to help participants acquire skills. By practicing positive customer service behaviors, participants can try out new ways of relating, receive feedback on their performances, watch others perform tasks, offer suggestions and encouragement, and repeat behaviors for skill development.

- **Games.** Games help people have fun. The games included in this book also have associated learning points that can be addressed in ways that suit your needs.

- **Individual activities.** These include written work and individual work. They are designed to help participants think about the concepts presented and discover ways to apply what they learn.

- **Icebreakers.** These activities are important at the beginning of a training program because they help warm the group up. They also can be used at other times to help people relax and to foster open communication.

- **Energizers.** Energizers help get the blood flowing and put zest into the program. They can be used anytime you think people need a change of format. Energizers usually include some physical component, such as getting people out of their seats to do a quick activity.

- **Structured experiences.** These are step-by-step activities that involve participants working together on an assignment. A crucial step in structured experiences is debriefing, during which participants review the learning that occurred as a result of involvement and observation.

Chapters 13 and 14 include a variety of learning activities that might be incorporated into your training, and suggestions for ways to combine independent activities, group exercises, energizers, icebreakers, and other learning methods. Because the intent of this program is to facilitate skill development, many of the exercises and activities build on each other.

Learning activities include brief presentations, or mini-lectures, to assist you in presenting and summarizing key points. You also will find descriptions of the sorts of comments you might hear, and suggestions about how to respond. Use the recommendations as you see fit, or provide your own commentary.

Each learning activity in chapters 13 and 14 includes

- goals

- materials

- timeframes

- instructions

- debriefing (when appropriate).

The program designs in chapters 7, 8, and 9 refer you to the learning activities suggested for use in those programs. Handouts for participants are included in the learning activities.

Slides that accompany the activities are gathered into ready-made PowerPoint presentations. On the CD the PowerPoint slides suggested for the one-hour program *(One-Hour.ppt)* are numbered 1 through 5. The slides suggested for the half-day program *(Half-Day.ppt)* are numbered 1 through 27. The slides suggested for the full-day program *(One-Day.ppt)* are numbered 1 through 46. In the book you'll find the slides for each of the three programs depicted at the ends of chapters 7, 8, and 9. The numbers identifying the slides in the book are the chapter number followed by the number of the slide for that program (for example, slide 7–1 in the book is slide 1 for the one-hour program on the CD).

You can use the PowerPoint presentations as they are, or you may choose slides to suit your customized content from the slides in each of the three program presentations. Open the program from which you'll be selecting slides *(One-Hour.ppt, Half-Day.ppt, or One-Day.ppt)* and copy it under another name. Then delete the slides you do not want to use in your presentation.

ASSESSMENT INSTRUMENTS

Assessment instruments for use in training sessions are provided in chapter 12. These assessments are designed to obtain reactions and responses, and to encourage reflection for professional growth. They are *not* intended to be validated instruments. Their purpose is to enable participants to reflect on their own opinions and behaviors, and to help determine areas in which they might improve.

Icons

For your easy reference, icons have been included in the outside margins of this workbook. They will help you identify key items in a chapter or activity, and easily locate handouts. Here is what the icons look like:

CD: Indicates materials included on the CD accompanying this workbook.

Activity: Appears when an agenda includes a learning activity and it identifies each learning activity presented.

Assessment: Appears when an agenda or learning activity includes an assessment and it identifies each assessment presented.

Clock: Indicates suggested timeframes for an activity.

Handout: Appears when an agenda or learning activity includes a handout. It indicates materials you can print or copy and use in ways that enhance the training experience.

Key Point: Will alert you to key points that should be emphasized in relation to a particular topic.

PowerPoint Item: Indicates PowerPoint presentations and slides that can be used individually. These presentations and slides are on the CD included with your workbook, and copies of the slides appear on pages 48, 55–59, and 70–76. Instructions for using PowerPoint slides and the CD are included in the appendix.

What to Do Next: Denotes recommendations for what to do after completing a particular section of this workbook.

What to Do Next

- ◆ Review the next chapter to learn about the theories that form the foundation for the activities in this workbook.

- ◆ Conduct any research of your own that will assist you in delivering your customer service training.

- ◆ Begin thinking about why customer service is important in your organization.

◆ ◆ ◆

The next chapter will introduce the Fantastic Service Equation, a tool you can use in developing your training programs. It also will explain the basic assumptions that underlie the Fantastic Service Every Time program.

The Fantastic Service Equation

This chapter introduces the Fantastic Service Equation, the foundation for the customer service training program presented in this workbook.

Theories of Motivation

What motivates people to provide good service? How do employees view customers? Do they see customers as uncooperative and unhelpful in the problem-solving process, or do they see them as active participants when presented with the right information and a positive attitude?

We might ask similar questions about staff. Do staff members believe that most of their colleagues are uncooperative, cynical, and don't want to give good customer service, or do they believe that, given the right tools, people will practice excellent customer service?

These questions might be answered by looking at motivational theory. In *The Human Side of Enterprise* (1960), psychologist Douglas McGregor described how different sets of assumptions, or theories, lead to two types of management styles. He labeled those two sets of assumptions Theory X and Theory Y. Theory X is the view that people will not work up to capacity unless they are directed, persuaded, punished, or controlled by an authority figure. Basically, it assumes that people are lazy and resistant, and that they won't work unless they are coerced.

Theory Y does not assume people are naturally passive or resistant to organizational needs. Rather, the theory is that people become idle and stagnant because of their experiences in organizations, not because they are inherently lazy. Proponents of Theory Y believe that, given the right circumstances, most people will harness their innate desire to succeed and work up to their potential.

This workbook takes Theory Y to be the better way of thinking of customer service interactions. That model encourages empowerment as an effective way to meet and exceed customer needs, and builds on employees' natural desires to assist customers. It also assumes that, given the right circumstances, most customers have a desire to be cooperative and loyal.

Customer Loyalty

Texas A&M University's Leonard Berry and his associates (1994) found there are five predominant factors that motivate customers to be loyal. Berry's findings have been used in customer service research by many organizations, and they provide the framework for popular books such as *Delivering Knock Your Socks Off Service,* by Kristin Anderson and Ron Zemke (1998).

The five main factors that influence customer loyalty are

1. **Reliability:** The capability to deliver the service that was promised, in a dependable and accurate way

2. **Responsiveness:** Eagerness to help customers and to deliver prompt service

3. **Assurance:** Employee skill, knowledge, and courtesy, and the ability to solve problems confidently and convey trust

4. **Empathy:** Caring, individual attention, and interest in building relationships with customers

5. **Tangibles:** Appearance of buildings, facilities, equipment, and communication materials.

You might think of these factors as part of a customer's hierarchy of needs, including the essentials (deliver what you promise) as well as higher order needs (deliver with care). This hierarchy is similar to Maslow's theory (1987) that people are motivated first by the basics, but also by more sophisticated needs such as self-esteem and self-actualization (for further discussion of this theory, see www.Maslow.com).

Another tool for considering customer loyalty is customer relationship management. CRM is a popular concept that focuses on building lifelong relationships with customers, and marketing products and services based on customer needs. The CRM model encourages doing what it takes to retain customers. This includes personalizing transactions as much as possible in order to gain loyalty. Personalizing increases the value an organization has to customers, and vice versa.

The Fantastic Service Equation

This workbook brings together years of observation and research on customer needs, and develops a Fantastic Service Equation (Figure 2–1) that puts theoretical knowledge into practice. The equation provides a framework for giving exceptional service to both internal customers and external customers every

Figure 2–1

The Fantastic Service Equation

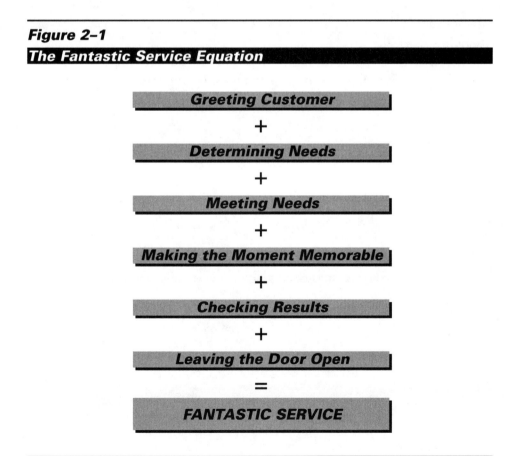

Greeting Customer

+

Determining Needs

+

Meeting Needs

+

Making the Moment Memorable

+

Checking Results

+

Leaving the Door Open

=

FANTASTIC SERVICE

time, and it provides a simple way to remember the essentials of good service. It will be referred to and expanded in other sections of this workbook, including Learning Activity 13–7: Fantastic Service Equation.

In addition to providing a foundation for training, the Fantastic Service Equation can be used in the workplace. For example, it can be used in staff meetings to discuss or demonstrate how participants are practicing the components of good service back on the job.

What to Do Next

- ◆ Become familiar with the Fantastic Service Equation.

- ◆ Choose your own stories or customer service experiences that will help illustrate the components of the Fantastic Service Equation.

- ◆ Conduct any research that you determine will be helpful.

- ◆ Read chapter 3, "Assessing the Organizational Need."

◆◆◆

The next chapter will discuss how to determine the needs of your organization so that you can design a suitable and effective program.

Assessing the Organizational Need

- Assessing organizational needs for a customer service program

- Strategic planning and the customer service initiative

Not all organizations are ready for customer service training. In fact, you can really stir up the pot if upper management is not supportive of training. Imagine this worst-case scenario: You do frontline training, get a great response, have people really enthusiastic about improving service, and then *wham!* They go back to their work environments and their managers say, "That won't work here!" Such a situation could be very demotivating.

To avoid that scenario, consider doing some research before you begin. Structured interviews, focus groups, surveys, and strategic needs assessments are all good ways to learn about the needs of an organization and to gain support for your training program.

Structured Interviews

Start structured interviews as high up in the organization as you can go, with the president if possible. Make sure that you include input from human resource personnel and line or operations managers and supervisors. Managers and supervisors will want to tell you what they have seen and what they consider the most pressing customer service issues in the organization.

The questions below can be useful when holding structured interviews with executives, but similar questions can be used for supervisors and employees. Asking these questions will elicit a lot of useful information. If the answers indicate that procedures, product knowledge, equipment, or concerns other than courtesy are problems, it would be beneficial to follow up on those issues with the appropriate departments.

If some procedures are not customer-friendly, training may be a catalyst for change. If change is not in the cards, the activities in this program will help employees overcome some of the obstacles they perceive by improving their communication skills.

STRUCTURED INTERVIEW QUESTIONS

1. What do you see as the major issues regarding customer service in your environment?

2. Do you have any way of measuring customer satisfaction?

3. How capable are your supervisors and managers of fielding customer service problems?

4. What customer service skills would you like to improve in your supervisory and management teams?

5. Do your organization's performance appraisals reflect customer service goals?

6. What frontline customer service skills would you like to see improved?

7. Do you have a mission statement?

8. On a scale of one to 10, how would you rate your organization on the following:

   ◆ the company's ability to provide what is promised

   ◆ the staff's willingness to help customers and to deliver prompt service

   ◆ employee knowledge about organizational procedures, products, and services

   ◆ courteous treatment of customers by employees

   ◆ courteous treatment of internal staff members by each other

   ◆ teamwork within departments

   ◆ teamwork between departments

   ◆ the aesthetic appearance of physical facilities

    ◆   adequate equipment for employees to accomplish your organization's mission.

  9. Would you be willing to set up an internal process to address empowerment initiatives?

10. Are you willing to discuss issues that arise in my interviews with your staff?

11. If you think it would help your customer service goals, would you be willing to make changes that employees recommend?

12. Would you like to empower your employees to make more decisions?

13. What would you like me to accomplish in the training process?

14. How can I be of most help to you?

Focus Groups

Focus groups can be set up to give people opportunities to brainstorm their ideas about customer service and to realize the potential of team involvement. One comment may spark another and so on. Focus groups should begin with questions that you prepare. Record responses and comments on a flipchart so everyone can see them. If that is not possible, you may simply take notes. Results of the sessions should be compiled.

Surveys

Needs analysis is another way to get information about how an organization's customer service is perceived. Structured interviews and focus groups are good resources for developing questions because they will allow you to see what trends emerge in discussions. A training needs survey can then quantify data with a broader population.

Strategic Needs Assessments

"Strategic partner" is a term that you probably have heard many times. Being a strategic partner means understanding where the organization is going in the future and helping it get there. It involves taking into account what leaders think is important regarding major outcomes and mission, and partnering to achieve those results. Any training that you provide needs to relate directly to those business goals and should be seen as advantageous to the bottom line.

An assessment of future directions usually identifies emerging issues and trends that will have a major effect on a business and its customers over a two- to three-year period. The assessment helps a business develop goals and programs that proactively anticipate and address the future, and position the organization to influence the future.

To conduct an assessment of the future, organizations look at such issues as expected changes within the business (these include changes in technology and professional requirements) and expected changes outside the company (these include major issues such as economy, demographics, politics, and the environment).

Results of an assessment provide a rationale for developing company and departmental goals and for making policy and budgetary decisions. From the assessment comes a summary of key change dynamics that will affect the business.

The following questions often are asked in strategic needs assessments:

- What information did previous organizational assessments impart?
- Are those issues and trends still relevant?
- Do the results point to what may need to be done differently in the future?
- How has the organization performed in achieving results?
- What is the present workforce like?
- How will it change or need to change?
- What does the organization know about future changes in customer needs?
- Are customer surveys conducted?
- What do the surveys say?
- How might the organization have to change to serve customers better?
- Is the company's organizational structure working to achieve results?
- What are the strengths and limitations of the company?
- What are the opportunities for positive change?

Figure 3–1
A SWOT Analysis Model

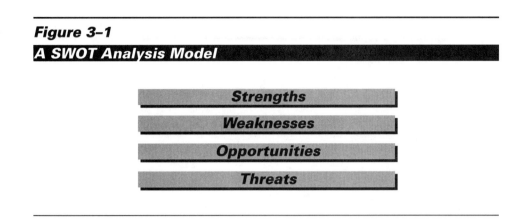

- **Strengths**
- **Weaknesses**
- **Opportunities**
- **Threats**

◆ What do your competitors do or say that might have implications for your organization?

◆ What are the most important opportunities for the future?

◆ What are the biggest problems?

◆ Is the organization in a competitive marketplace?

◆ How does the organization compare with competitors?

The results can be summarized in a SWOT analysis model (see Figure 3–1). Action plans are then developed to increase the **S**trengths, overcome the **W**eaknesses, plan for the **O**pportunities, and decrease the **T**hreats. For more information on strategic planning, see chapter 10.

What to Do Next

◆ Review the pros and cons of using the methods described for assessing organizational needs, based on time factors, organizational commitment, resources, and expertise.

◆ Choose the methods you will use to determine the organization's customer service training needs.

◆ Follow up with leaders.

◆ Review training alternatives with organizational leaders.

◆◆◆

After you have assessed the needs of your organization, the next chapter will assist you in designing a training program.

Designing Your Training

- ◆ Learning concepts
- ◆ Training designs
- ◆ Advantages of different designs

This chapter provides some background to help you choose a training design that fits the needs and time limitations of your organization.

Developing Training Designs

The purpose of your training is to help people learn how to provide excellent customer service. There are many different ways to achieve this goal, and so a crucial step is deciding how you will help learners see the relevance of the material you present. The instructional process involves preparing learning opportunities and considering how activities will appeal to different types of learners.

The program designs in the following chapters include curriculum guidelines for training sessions. If you have completed some assessment to determine the actual needs and goals of your organization (as described in the previous chapter), you will have a better idea of which programs or learning activities will best meet your needs.

Learning is a very individual process. Chapter 5 highlights some principles of adult learning and facilitation that will help you think about how to enhance the learning process. In addition, some information from basic learning theory might help you design a suitable curriculum.

In her book *About Learning*, Berenice McCarthy (1996) suggests that people learn in the following four ways:

1. There are those who ask "Why?" and who need to reflect in concrete ways, such as asking questions and writing.

2. There are those who ask "What?" and who need to know theories, facts, expert opinions, and history. They are more receptive to texts and lectures.

3. There are those who ask "How?" and who like to know the experimental background and laboratory steps involved in coming to conclusions.

4. There are those who ask "So what?" and who need to see the practical implications and results, and how information fits their experiences.

In addition to asking different questions, learners also receive information in different ways. Some learn best by hearing (auditory), some learn best by seeing (visual), and some learn best by doing (kinesthetic). A good repertoire of instructional activities includes methods that appeal to different learning styles. To get an idea of your own learning style, you can take the Learning Styles Modality Preference Inventory on the Middlesex Community College Website (www.mxctc.commnet.edu/clc/survey.htm).

For a comprehensive discussion of learning theory and instructional design, *Principles of Instructional Design* by Gagne, Briggs, and Wager (1992) is an excellent reference. Of course, factors such as attitude, intellectual skills, and motor skills also affect learning.

The activities in this workbook appeal to learners with different modalities. They include handouts, research references, and PowerPoint slides to read; quiet time to write notes and reflect; opportunities for listening and talking; and exercises for practicing skills.

Establishing a Framework

To help trainees understand the goals of training, and how material relates to real work situations, it is helpful to establish a framework. In presenting a framework, trainers should provide an overview of why the training is taking place and why it is important. This explanation should address the reasons a specific organization has decided to undertake customer service training. It also should highlight what the trainer hopes to accomplish, and how the skills learned in this training will be useful back on the job.

Goals of the programs and learning activities are described in this workbook, and you can use those when discussing the purposes of specific exercises. Many of the handouts will also help provide a framework for participants.

IDENTIFYING BEHAVIORS

"Improve customer service" is a broad goal. Within that goal are many behaviors that make up the human relations component of good customer service. For example, listening and giving clear directions are behaviors that are necessary for good customer service. One does not improve customer service simply because he or she is told to do so—participants need to understand the reasons and see the relevant parts of the equation. For these reasons, relevant behaviors will be identified and discussed throughout the program.

Training helps people identify the behaviors that are important for good customer service, so that those behaviors might be improved. Learning activities enable participants to analyze different skills and behaviors, and separate the parts from the whole.

PRACTICING

Practice is crucial for learning because learning takes place by doing and by seeing. In the training designs included in this workbook, practice occurs in written exercises, verbal exercises, and role playing. Role playing helps participants actually practice the behaviors that are being addressed. Role-play exercises bring skills and behaviors to life for those acting particular roles and for those observing the scenarios.

PROVIDING FEEDBACK

A key aspect of training is the feedback trainers give to participants. If delivered in a supportive and constructive manner, your feedback will help learners develop a deeper understanding of the content you are presenting and the behaviors they are practicing. Feedback in role plays is especially powerful because this is when "the rubber hits the road." In role plays, observers can see if people are able to practice the behaviors that have been discussed, or whether habitual responses will prevail.

It takes a lot of practice to learn a new skill. Some participants will learn skills more quickly than others. Some people's attitudes might prevent them from being open to trying new behaviors. Your job is to facilitate the session to the best of your ability, and to take different learning styles into account. The rest is up to the participants.

MAKING IT RELEVANT

Throughout the program you will be discussing how to use skills and new behaviors on the job. These discussions will help answer the question "So what?" Exercises and action plans also will help participants bring new skills back to actual work situations.

The Designs in This Workbook

There are several designs to choose from in this workbook. You also can mix and match activities and incorporate your own activities into the designs included here. There are many ways to turn structured experiences into games or to add different dimensions to activities by using your own creative touch.

ONE-DAY PROGRAM

A full-day program gives you the time to cover customer service concepts in more depth than a half-day or one-hour program. It also enables you to

- ◆ determine the needs of learners

- ◆ use all learning modalities

- ◆ concentrate on meeting the needs of participants

- ◆ provide ample time for discussion

- ◆ practice more concepts

- ◆ build on each skill in the Fantastic Service Equation

- ◆ conduct role plays

- ◆ provide feedback

- ◆ take time for "instant replays"

- ◆ facilitate action plans for taking what is learned back to work.

A sample one-day program is provided in chapter 9. There also are optional learning activities in chapter 14 that you can substitute into the design that is presented (and you can incorporate your own exercises). The one-day program uses all the components of the Fantastic Service Equation. If you use the one-day program in chapter 9, the sample agenda of approximate times will give you an idea of how the program flows.

You also can split this full-day program into two sessions, facilitating the first part on the first day and the second part on another day. This works well for organizations that cannot afford to have all customer service personnel away from their customers for a full day. It also gives participants time to practice skills between sessions and to share their successes during the second part of the program.

HALF-DAY PROGRAM

The half-day session presented in this workbook (chapter 8) is a condensed version of the one-day program. You may choose to use this version if

- time does not allow for a one-day program

- budget constraints prohibit a full day of training

- the goal is quickly to increase many participants' awareness of the importance of excellent customer service.

ONE-HOUR PROGRAM

The one-hour program (chapter 7) provides an introduction to customer service and to the Fantastic Service Equation. Depending on your needs, you could use various exercises for a one-day program; the agenda suggested is only an example. It also is possible to run a number of one-hour workshops as a series of scheduled training events. This can even occur at brown-bag lunches or staff meetings.

You might run a one-hour training if

- your organization wants to offer a quick program

- you are asked to do a short program for a specific event

- the budget is limited

- time away from work is an issue.

What to Do Next

- Review program options and the pros and cons of the one-hour, half-day, and one-day programs.

- ◆ Determine if you will be using the plan as it appears in this workbook, modifying an existing plan, or creating an entirely new design.

- ◆ Choose a program that best suits the organization's customer service training needs.

- ◆ Follow up with organizational leaders to confirm that they will support your choice.

◆◆◆

The next chapter gives practical suggestions regarding how to facilitate the program you choose, what to keep in mind when working with adult learners, and how to prepare for your training.

Chapter 5

Facilitating the Training Session

What's in This Chapter?

- Facilitation tips

- Discussion of adult learning theory

- Pointers on being prepared for your trainings

- Planning suggestions

Everyone thinks she or he is an expert in customer service. Because this program aims at helping participants learn how to make the customer feel right, respected, and appreciated, it is important to make *your customers,* the participants, feel that their contributions are respected and valued. This involves focusing on what each participant contributes to the discussion, and anticipating how you can work with comments that are right, wrong, semi-right, and semi-wrong, and how you can make all contributions count.

The more participation you elicit during class, the better your results will be. The more active participation you create (and facilitating *is* a creative activity), the more people will buy into the program, and the more they will learn. Most important, the more people participate, the more likely it is that they actually will use the skills you are teaching.

Learning activities include short presentations of conceptual material. However, the program emphasizes active involvement through individual work, work in pairs and small groups, and total class involvement. Participatory exercises give the people who like to talk in groups opportunities to present their ideas, and enable those who do not like to express their opinions in large groups do individual work or converse with a partner. Your facilitation of these activities is the key to the success of the program.

Adult Learning Theory

Because training is a matter of teaching adults, it will be helpful to brush up on adult learning principles, and to highlight the aspects of learning theory that apply to a customer service training program.

Most training involves a mixed-age group of adults. It is helpful to remember that adult learners want to be involved in their learning. Good facilitation skills will help learners get involved. Below are some important points to be aware of when working with adult learners.

Adult learners...

- ◆ need to relate their own experiences to new material and make connections to things that are familiar. They often need to tell you what they know, or what they have learned by experience.

- ◆ usually want educational experiences that relate to real-life situations. They retain the most when they can put their learning to immediate use, and prefer dealing with realistic and practical examples and situations.

- ◆ often are issue-centered or problem-centered rather than subject-centered.

- ◆ are diverse. In addition to cultural differences, they have different learning styles and take different amounts of time when completing exercises.

- ◆ may not have been in a classroom setting in many years, or may need some time to adjust to a new learning environment. They may not be used to a learning context in which their comments are welcomed and where they don't have to raise their hands or perform other traditional school tasks.

- ◆ are sensitive to what they might perceive as failure in a learning environment. They may be fearful that they will be unable to learn new things.

- ◆ may think they know it all already, and can find it difficult to change opinions and perceptions.

Facilitation

At the beginning of each customer service training session, it will be beneficial for you to describe the difference between a lecturer and facilitator, and to let participants know that your role is to facilitate. Emphasize that you are there to assist them in learning from each other and from exercises and concepts that will enhance their knowledge and expand their thinking about customer service. It is important to recognize at the outset that participants' experiences are important sources of knowledge.

As a facilitator, you will

- work with some principles participants already know

- encourage participants to share their good customer service practices

- recognize the results that participants have already achieved in their work environments

- provide a systematic way to view customer service, so as to encourage awareness of the behaviors that produce even better results

- focus the discussion

- keep timeframes

- encourage participation from all members

- set a positive tone

- lead by example.

Everyone has his or her own facilitation style. Facilitation is an art form, much like dancing or playing in a jazz band. In dancing, you have to have a rhythm with your partner. With jazz, a player improvises on the melody of a song without straying too far from the underlying form and harmonic content.

ELEMENTS OF SUCCESSFUL FACILITATION

It would be impossible to describe all the elements of good facilitation, but here are some essentials:

- Make people feel welcome.

- Greet people and find out their names as they walk into class.

- Ask questions.

- Listen to responses.

- Paraphrase responses.

- When recording responses on a flipchart, write down as exactly as possible what was said.

- Wait for responses while people think—be comfortable with some silence.

- Positively reinforce whatever you can.

- Turn imperfect responses into better ones and reinforce the contributor's efforts.

- Be enthusiastic.

- Smile.

- Maintain good eye contact and look at one person at a time when you are speaking.

- Use your sense of humor.

- Encourage everyone to participate.

- Focus the discussion.

- Invite participants with questions not relevant to the whole class to talk with you during the break.

- Summarize what people say.

- Summarize discussions.

- Review principles as you work through the program.

- Compliment the group often (as appropriate).

- Be clear and to the point when delivering content.

- Give clear directions and repeat them whenever necessary.

- Use ideas from the group to make points included in the program.

- Use people's names.

- Limit how long you talk.

USEFUL RESPONSES

To focus the discussion, make comments such as these:

- ◆ "Let's get back to our original question."

- ◆ "Thanks for that example. We're going to highlight some of those issues next."

To limit a marathon talker, try this strategy:

- ◆ "Thanks, Mary—what do the rest of you think?"

To turn imperfect responses into better ones, make an alternate suggestion:

- ◆ "How about this . . . ?"

To compliment and encourage the whole group, give this kind of feedback:

- ◆ "You really know a lot about this!"

- ◆ "What great ideas!"

Being Prepared

Anyone who has ever trained a class knows how crucial preparation is to the end result. As trainers also know, after you have run a training session once, it is much easier to run subsequent sessions.

KNOWING YOUR AUDIENCE

You may or may not be able to determine who comes to training. Your audience will depend on your client and your client's goals. It is always a boost if you can start training at an executive level. If you can do an executive overview, you will have greater credibility when your participants ask the inevitable question, "Have our executives done this training?" The ideal situation is to train executives, managers, and supervisors before training frontline workers.

It is always helpful to know something about the job responsibilities of the people who will be attending training. You don't need to be an expert, but it is good to be somewhat familiar with the work worlds of participants. If you are an in-house trainer, you might observe people in different settings or conduct focus groups. If you are a consultant or contract trainer, you might spend some time observing workers at your client's facility or conduct focus groups.

Because this program is so highly interactive, it works best with 15 to 25 participants. Fewer than 15 may not give you the interaction needed for camaraderie and discussion. More than 25 can be too much of a good thing. Room availability is usually an issue, and most organizations do not have a training room that accommodates more than 25 people.

INVITING PARTICIPANTS

Whenever possible, arrange for invitations to your training to come from a top executive or someone in a leadership position. In *The ASTD Trainer's Sourcebook* (1996), Elaine Beich notes the fact that invitations peak the interest of trainees more effectively than do memos stating, "You will come to training and like it!"

How many times have you asked participants why they are at a particular workshop, and heard the reply, "We were sent here. We all got the memo"? That method of recruitment is a good way to get a lot of hostile people together in one room, with one goal: Get the trainer.

The best scenario is to prepare an invitation, or have an executive write an invitation, and to have each participant meet with his or her boss to discuss what areas of your training will be most important for him or her. If you get the opportunity to train higher level leaders, you can make this suggestion during their training.

There are many ways to market your training. You can send preview cards that read, "You are the Key to Customer Service. Come to the workshop on this date and find out how important you are to customers." You can tie balloons reading, "I'm important—I'm celebrating my customer service skills in training class!" to the desks of people who are in training. You can create buttons with a customer service slogan for people who attend class. Depending on your budget, there are many things you can do to promote and reinforce training.

Another way to announce training plans is to have a kickoff ceremony to introduce the customer service theme. This can be a short ceremony that occurs in a division, department, unit, or at whatever level your organization recommends.

Many companies inform people about training through training calendars, newsletters, email, fliers, or other methods. There may be internal procedures for people to follow to sign up and receive confirmations.

ORGANIZING THE DETAILS

Training professionals have different ways of preparing for classes, and you may do what has been most successful for you. Timeframes for preparation are difficult to determine because they depend on when training is requested and how much time is available for preparation. Needless to say, the sooner you can attend to the details, the more time you actually will have to work with the material and make it your own. Below is a guide for preparing your program in a thorough and timely fashion.

Things to do at least a month before your training:

◆ Determine the dates and times of training, the number of participants, and the training site.

◆ Specify how you want the room arranged (unless you will be doing that yourself the day of training). Recommended room arrangements for this program are a U-shape or round tables with four to six people per table.

◆ Order the audiovisual equipment, and be sure to have a table for your materials and equipment.

◆ Decide if you will use music in the session for background or breaks, and if you want to use chimes or other musical instruments to indicate when times for activities are nearing a close or are up.

◆ With your organization, decide if you will have food or beverages for breaks or lunch for the full-day program. Order the food and drinks.

◆ Order the materials that you will need for trainers and participants.

Ordering materials for participants:

◆ Send out invitations or announcements.

◆ If necessary, obtain a map or directions to the training site, and send the map to participants.

◆ Order pens and tent cards or name tags.

◆ Order certificates if you will be using them, and any other gifts or prizes you will be giving out.

◆ Create or obtain a sign-in sheet.

◆ Create or obtain evaluation forms.

Ordering materials for trainers:

- Decide on the material that you want to use for the training program.

- Arrange a time for the material to be duplicated and bound.

- Determine how those materials will get to the training site.

- Create or review transparencies and PowerPoint presentations.

- Order marking pens.

- Order flipchart paper.

- Order masking tape.

Things to do a week or two before the session:

- Review the program several times.

- Make notes of customer service stories and examples that will reinforce the concepts in the training.

- Go through the flow of the session and get a clear picture of how you want it to go.

- Be sure the books and handouts are in order.

- Prepare flipcharts.

Things to do the day of the session:

- Get these program materials to the training room:

  - books

  - flipchart stand with full pad of paper

  - masking tape

  - CD or tape player (optional)

  - music (optional)

  - chimes or other musical instruments (optional)

  - overhead projector or laptop and LCD projector

  - screen

- ♦ extension cord and powerstrip

- ♦ videos (optional)

- ♦ marking pens

- ♦ sign-in sheets

- ♦ evaluations

- ♦ water (for you or for everyone)

- ♦ Get to the site at least one hour before the training starts.

- ♦ Set up the training room.

- ♦ Put a name tag and book at each place.

- ♦ Put marking pens on tables for people to fill out name tags.

- ♦ Set up equipment, including video monitor, PowerPoint/LCD, overhead projector, and screen.

- ♦ Set up flipchart.

- ♦ Welcome participants as they come in and introduce yourself to each participant.

What to Do Next

- ♦ Determine the number of participants and the length of your training program.

- ♦ Choose a site.

- ♦ Make arrangements and order materials.

- ♦ Follow up with planning recommendations.

- ♦ Invite participants to your training.

♦ ♦ ♦

The next chapter will help you determine how best to evaluate your training program.

Evaluating Learning

- ◆ Purposes of evaluation

- ◆ Levels of measurement and evaluation

- ◆ Program evaluation options

This chapter will give you some ideas about how to evaluate your training program. Evaluation of results will depend on what you are looking for in terms of benefits to participants and to the organization.

Purposes of Evaluation

There are many ways to evaluate training. The purpose of your evaluation will determine the evaluation methods you use.

Before training begins, determine the purpose of evaluating your program. In fact, this is a useful subject to address with organizational leaders. Trainers often begin a program without thinking about how the program fits into a strategic plan or how it supports and promotes specific business goals. The discussion in chapter 3 on assessing strategic needs addresses how a customer service program might match larger business goals and support the organization's mission and vision. Talking with influential leaders about how you will evaluate your customer service program will encourage them to buy into the program. It also will heighten the visibility of training and help create partnerships within different areas of the organization.

LEVELS OF MEASUREMENT

Donald Kirkpatrick (1977), one of the leading experts in measuring training results, identified four levels of measurement and evaluation. Deciding which of these four levels are most important to you will help you determine the purpose of your evaluation and the methods you might use to conduct it.

- **Level I—Reaction:** Measures how participants react to the training event.

- **Level II—Learning:** Evaluates whether participants have learned and understood the content of training.

- **Level III—Behavior:** Measures changes in behavior and actual and perceived improvements in performance.

- **Level IV—Results:** Evaluates the impact of training on the bottom line.

These four levels correspond with the evaluation methods described below.

EVALUATION METHODS

Evaluating Participant Reactions

One of the most common ways trainers measure participants' reactions is by administering end-of-session evaluation forms. Although they are frequently used, evaluation forms have inherent limitations. Participants may lack perspective on the effectiveness of training techniques. In addition, results can be overly influenced by the personality of the facilitator or participants' feelings about having to attend training. Before you rely on evaluation forms, you might want to read the article "Don't Smile About Smile Sheets" by John E. Jones (1990).

Evaluation forms are used so frequently because they are easy to administer. If you choose this method, consider the suggestions below. Additional tips on creating evaluation forms are found in the book *Figuring Things Out: A Trainer's Guide to Needs and Task Analysis* by Zemke and Kramlinger (1987).

Here are a few suggestions for creating evaluation forms:

- Make your questions brief.

- Leave adequate space for comments.

- Group types of questions into categories (for example, cluster together questions about content, questions about the instructor, and questions about materials).

◆ Provide variety in types of questions (include multiple-choice, true-false, short-answer, and open-ended items).

◆ Include relevant decision makers in your questionnaire design.

◆ Plan how you will use and analyze the data and create a design that will facilitate your analysis.

◆ Use positively worded items (such as, "I listen to others," instead of "I don't listen to others").

Measuring the Extent to Which Participants Have Learned and Understood the Content of Training

If you want to determine the extent to which participants have understood the content of your customer service program, testing is an option. Comparing pretraining and posttraining test results will give you an indication of the amount of knowledge gained. Or you can give a quiz that tests conceptual information 30 to 60 days after the training to see if people remember the concepts. Because most adult learners do not generally like the idea of tests, you might want to refer to these evaluations as "assessments."

Measuring the Results of Training Back on the Job

Methods for collecting data regarding performance back on the job include reports by people who manage participants, reports from staff and peers, observations, quality monitors, and other quality and efficiency measures.

Measuring the Organizational Impact of Training

Measuring organizational impact requires working with leaders to create and implement a plan to collect the data you need. Possible methods include customer surveys, measurements of sales, studies of customer retention or turnover, employee satisfaction surveys, and other measurements of issues pertinent to the organization.

Robert Brinkerhoff, well-known author and researcher of evaluation methods, has suggested the following method to obtain information relevant to results:

1. Send out questionnaires to people who have gone through training. In these questionnaires ask, "To what extent have you used your training in a way that has made a significant business impact?" (This question can elicit information that will point to business benefits and ways to use other data to measure accomplishments.)

2. When you get responses back, conduct interviews to get more information.

Program Evaluation

The timing of when and how you measure results can help you improve your initial program. It is advisable to do both formative and summative evaluation to hone your program to meet learning objectives. Formative evaluation involves getting feedback during the initial phases. Summative evaluation will help you assess the whole program after you have completed training.

FORMATIVE EVALUATION

Formative evaluation involves conducting the program and using feedback to make changes that improve receptivity and relevance. Formative evaluation is an ongoing process that can include reviewing participant reactions and assessments, interviewing participants, and even asking for feedback during training sessions. For example, if participants say that they would like more time for certain activities or that they would like to do more group exercises, you can go back to your schedule and rearrange things accordingly.

Another way to do formative evaluation is to watch the role plays the class performs. You will notice areas of weakness when participants role play the concepts you have been instructing and discussing. For example, if participants do not make eye contact or demonstrate an enthusiastic greeting in role playing customer scenarios, you will see that this is an area that needs more attention, and so you might do more meet-and-greet exercises in future sessions.

SUMMATIVE EVALUATION

Summative evaluations usually are conducted after training is completed. The purpose of summative evaluation is to draw conclusions about how well the training worked. This type of evaluation is summative because it sums up all the evidence you have collected about the effects of training at various levels. It should answer the question, "In what ways and to what degree is this organization better as a result of the training?"

Summative evaluations can help you determine

◆ whether the customer training program should be part of ongoing training initiatives in the organization

- whether all new hires should participate in training

- whether follow-up training is needed

- whether other groups should receive training.

RETURN-ON-INVESTMENT

Measuring return-on-investment (ROI) is useful and can help "sell" training to leaders. Jack J. Phillips' *Handbook of Training Evaluation and Measurement Methods* (1983) is a good resource for learning ROI methods. To calculate ROI, you need to know how much money is being spent on training, and what is being gained by the organization as a result of the training. Information about your organization's ROI can help leaders decide whether to conduct a training program.

Because this workbook includes many different exercises, and you probably will include your own exercises in your training, it is advisable to test the waters with a pilot program before you implement your program more broadly.

What to Do Next

- Review the program objectives and designs and the learning activities in the following chapters.

- Clarify the objectives for your program.

- Determine how you will evaluate your program and how you will acquire the necessary data.

◆ ◆ ◆

When you have determined the training needs of your organization and how you will evaluate the results of your training, you will need to determine the type, length, and content of the program you will use. The following chapters include sample designs.

◆

One-Hour Program

- ◆ Design for a one-hour training program
- ◆ Purpose and objectives of the program
- ◆ Instructions for how to conduct the unit
- ◆ Program agenda

This chapter includes a short program that can be used as an introduction for a customer service initiative, as a stand-alone unit, or as part of a staff meeting. Some of the exercises in this session also are included in the more comprehensive half-day and one-day programs.

Training Objectives

- ◆ Recognize team behaviors that contribute to fantastic customer service.
- ◆ Identify negative service behaviors.
- ◆ Practice listening.
- ◆ Identify behaviors that constitute fantastic service.
- ◆ Individually assess positive behaviors.

Materials

For the instructor:

- ◆ This chapter for reference notes
- ◆ Learning Activity 13–1: Skills Analysis
- ◆ Learning Activity 13–7: Fantastic Service Equation

♦ PowerPoint slides: "Your Worst Customer Service Experience," "Caring Is the Greatest Gift," and "Fantastic Service Equation" (slides 7–1 through 7–5 on page 48). To access slides for this program, open the file *One-Hour.ppt* on the accompanying CD. Copies of the slides for this training session are included at the end of this chapter.

For the participants:

♦ Handout 13–5: The Fantastic Service Equation

♦ Assessment 12–3: Fantastic Service Every Time Survey

Using the CD

Materials for this training session are provided in this workbook and as electronic files on the accompanying CD. To access the electronic files, insert the CD and click on the appropriate Adobe .pdf document. Further directions and help locating and using the files can be found in the appendix, "Using the Compact Disc."

One-Hour Sample Agenda: Fantastic Service Every Time

8:00 a.m.   Welcome (5 minutes)

Welcome participants to the program, introduce yourself, and provide background about why this program is being offered and what the sponsoring organization hopes to accomplish.

8:05   Learning Activity 13–1: Skills Analysis (10 minutes)

Facilitate Learning Activity 13–1: Skills Analysis (chapter 13, page 107). This exercise introduces customer service skills and provides the group with an opportunity for quick team building.

8:15   Roles, Responsibilities, and Objectives (5 minutes)

Describe your role, participant roles, and the objectives of the workshop. Encourage everyone to practice positive intent, keep an open mind, and think about how the concepts they will be learning might apply back at work.

8:20   Worst Customer Service Experience (15 minutes)

This exercise is part of Learning Activity 13–6: Moments of Truth (chapter 13, page 129), which is included in the one-day program. For the one-hour program, conduct the exercise as follows.

Tell participants that sometimes it is helpful to think of their own customer service experiences to get an idea of how other people might feel when they receive poor service.

Show the "Worst Customer Service" slide (slide 7–2).

Give these directions: *"I would like you to think of your own customer service experiences and how you as a customer might have received poor service at one time or another. The experience should be outside of your work environment (at an insurance company, restaurant, bank, or elsewhere)."*

Tell the participants they will be pairing up with partners to describe their worst customer service experiences. They each will have two minutes to describe their situations. Partners will take turns describing and listening. Instruct them to share the following details:

- ◆ your worst customer service experience in recent months

- ◆ what took place

- ◆ how the service provider(s) treated you

- ◆ your response

- ◆ the likelihood that you will return there

- ◆ how many people you told about the incident.

Call time after two minutes and ask that pairs switch roles. After five minutes, bring the group back together.

Ask what behaviors annoyed them as customers. Encourage specificity, and record responses on a flipchart.

Summarize the exercise by saying that the behaviors that they identified are not simply behaviors that *they* do not like—they are behaviors that no customer would like. Ask them what kinds of behaviors they would like to see.

Show the "Caring Is the Greatest Gift" slide (slide 7–3), to reinforce how important caring behaviors are in customer service environments.

8:35   Fantastic Service Equation (5 minutes)

Facilitate Learning Activity 13–7: Fantastic Service Equation (chapter 13, page 134). Explain that the Fantastic Service Equation is a framework for positive customer service behaviors such as those they just described.

Show the "Fantastic Service Equation" slide (slide 7-4), or write the Fantastic Service Equation on a flipchart.

Distribute and discuss Handout 13–5: The Fantastic Service Equation (chapter 13, page 135, or open the file *Handout 13–5.pdf* on the CD). Describe how the participants in this training session practiced the following actions in their beginning exercise (skills analysis).

1. **Greeting.** Greeted each other with eye contact and body language.

2. **Determining needs.** Practiced listening, which is one way to determine needs.

3. **Meeting needs.** Practiced problem solving in a quick and efficient manner.

4. **Checking results.** Checked for time and quality at the end of the exercise.

5. **Leaving the door open.** Remained open to questions and new information. To illustrate what it means to "leave the door open," you might tell participants that you will be available to answer questions for a few minutes after class.

8:40   Assessment (5 minutes)

Distribute Assessment 12–3: Fantastic Service Every Time
Survey (chapter 12, page 100, or open the file *Assessment
12–3.pdf* on the CD). Tell participants that they will be
assessing how well they practice the Fantastic Service
Equation with customers at work. Tell them that it is a
personal assessment and not a test, and that some items
may be more essential than others in their particular
jobs. Give participants at least five minutes to fill out the
assessment.

8:45   Assessment Discussion (15 minutes)

Ask participants how they would like to improve in the
areas they recorded on their assessments. Have volunteers share their improvement areas or have participants
pair up with partners or form trios to discuss.

9:00   Close

What to Do Next

- ◆ Prepare for the one-hour session.

- ◆ Compile the learning activities, assessments, handouts, and slides
  you will use in your training.

- ◆ Determine the schedule for training classes.

◆ ◆ ◆

The next chapter gives you an example of a half-day program.

Slide 7–1

Welcome to

Fantastic Service Every Time

Maxine Kamin, M.Ed.
American Society for Training & Development

Copyright 2002 Maxine Kamin   Fantastic Service Every Time

Slide 7–2

Your Worst Customer Service Experience...

Copyright 2002 Maxine Kamin   Fantastic Service Every Time

Slide 7–3

Caring Is the Greatest Gift

In these days of fast companies, desktop overload, and "press 1" for service, we are all looking for a little comfort — an act of kindness to get us through the day. Caring is the greatest gift we can give someone.

It is immeasurable.

Copyright 2002 Maxine Kamin   Fantastic Service Every Time

Slide 7–4

Fantastic Service Equation

Greeting the Customer +
Determining Needs +
Meeting Needs +
Making the Moment Memorable +
Checking Results +
Leaving the Door Open +

= Fantastic Service

Copyright 2002 Maxine Kamin   Fantastic Service Every Time

Slide 7–5

Be Caring and
Have Fun Out There!

Thanks for attending
Fantastic Service Every Time

Copyright 2002 Maxine Kamin   Fantastic Service Every Time

Half-Day Program

- Design for a half-day workshop
- Purpose and objectives of the program
- Notes on delivery and transitions
- Program agenda

This chapter provides you with a sample format for a half-day customer service training program. You may use the format as is or create your own half-day session by choosing different activities from chapters 13 or 14 or combining workbook activities with your own.

The half-day program is popular in organizations that cannot devote a full day to training but whose leaders are committed to spending half a day of quality time for training to improve customer service.

The advantages of the half-day program are that it delivers a message about excellent customer service and includes role plays so participants get a chance to practice the skills they learn in class. Another advantage is that you can run two half-day sessions back-to-back with different groups of trainees, allowing as many as 50 people to be trained in one day.

The half-day program is not as comprehensive as the full-day course and does not allow for as much skill practice before participants actually do the role plays. However, it provides a good start for training.

Training Objectives

- Recognize levels of service.
- Identify common customer expectations.

- Identify behaviors that constitute fantastic service.

- Practice effective listening skills.

- Use positive language.

- Practice problem solving.

- Demonstrate the Fantastic Service Equation.

Materials

For the instructor:

- This chapter for reference notes

- Learning Activity 13–1: Skills Analysis

- Learning Activity 13–3: Customer Expectations

- Learning Activity 13–7: Fantastic Service Equation

- Learning Activity 13–8: Greeting Group

- Learning Activity 13–9: Determining Needs: Communication

- Learning Activity 13–12: Positive Language

- Learning Activity 13–14: Meeting Needs: Problem Solving

- Learning Activity 13–16: Putting It All Together: Role Playing

- PowerPoint presentation: Half-Day. To access slides for this program, open the file *Half-Day.ppt* on the accompanying CD. Copies of the slides for this training session are included at the end of this chapter.

For the participants:

- Handout 13–1: Categories of Customer Expectations

- Handout 13–5: The Fantastic Service Equation

- Handout 13–6: Listening

- Handout 13–7: Paraphrase the Thought, Validate the Heart

- Handout 13–8: Positive Language

- Handout 13–10: Problem Solving

◆   Handout 13–11: Final Equation Components

◆   Any prizes you want to give out (optional)

◆   Food (optional)

Using the CD

Materials for this training session are provided in this workbook and as electronic files on the accompanying CD. To access the electronic files, insert the CD and click on the appropriate Adobe .pdf document. Further directions and help locating and using the files can be found in the appendix, "Using the Compact Disc."

Half-Day Sample Agenda: Fantastic Service Every Time

The times assigned to the elements of this training are approximate and will vary with discussion and trainer emphasis.

8:00 a.m.   Welcome (5 minutes)

Welcome participants to the program, introduce yourself, and provide background about why this program is being offered and what the sponsoring organization hopes to accomplish.

8:05   Learning Activity 13–1: Skills Analysis (10 minutes)

Facilitate Learning Activity 13–1: Skills Analysis (chapter 13, page 107). This exercise introduces customer service skills and provides the group with an opportunity for quick team building.

8:15   Roles, Responsibilities, and Objectives (5 minutes)

Describe your role, participant roles, and the objectives of the workshop (you might write the objectives on a flipchart and briefly go over them). Encourage everyone to practice positive intent, keep an open mind, and think about how the concepts they will be learning might apply back at work.

8:20   Learning Activity 13–3: Customer Expectations (chapter 13, page 114) (35 minutes)

Use the following team variation of this learning activity for discussion of assessment items because this will be the first time people will have an opportunity to get to know each other.

Put people in teams. Have each team come up with the five items they would describe as the most important customer needs. Have each team list their top five items on a piece of flipchart paper, and then draw a symbol or picture that depicts those needs. Have the teams choose a leader to present. After the first team reports, ask each member of that team to introduce himself or herself with the following details:

◆   name

◆   unit in the organization where participant works

◆   the one need that is most important to the participant as a customer

◆   one customer need that the participant feels he or she meets best

◆   one customer need that the participant could improve.

Repeat for each team.

8:55   Learning Activity 13–7: Fantastic Service Equation (chapter 13, page 134) (10 minutes)

Introduce the Fantastic Service Equation as a framework for identifying constructive customer service behaviors and for meeting the kinds of needs you have been discussing.

9:05   Learning Activity 13–8: Greeting Group (chapter 13, page 137) (5 minutes)

Highlight the importance of first impressions and greetings and have everyone greet each other nonverbally.

Emphasize that greeting is the first component of the Fantastic Service Equation.

9:10   Learning Activity 13–9: Determining Needs: Communication (chapter 13, page 139) (45 minutes)

Facilitate this activity to give participants an opportunity to practice communication skills, with an emphasis on listening, paraphrasing, and empathizing.

9:55   Break (15 minutes)

10:10   Learning Activity 13–12: Positive Language (chapter 13, page 152) (20 minutes)

Stress the importance of using positive language in the communication process to focus on what you *can* do instead of what you *can't* do.

10:30   Learning Activity 13–14: Meeting Needs: Problem Solving (chapter 13, page 161) (15 minutes)

Review guidelines for problem solving, using a participant example to work through the steps.

10:45   Learning Activity 13–16: Putting It All Together: Role Playing (chapter 13, page 166) (60 minutes)

Help participants develop role-play scenarios that will put together everything they have learned in the session. Role playing reinforces new behaviors. Participants often say this is one of the most valuable components of the program.

11:45   Conclusion and Evaluation (15 minutes)

Conclude the day by asking what participants learned, what they liked, what they would change, or any other questions you find productive. If you are planning to use evaluations, distribute them and thank the group for their attention.

Noon   Close

What to Do Next

◆ Prepare for the half-day session.

◆ Compile the learning activities, assessments, handouts, and slides you will use in your training.

◆ Determine the schedule for training classes.

◆◆◆

The following chapter includes an agenda and suggested learning activities for a full-day program.

Slide 8-1

Welcome to

Fantastic Service Every Time

Maxine Kamin, M.Ed.
American Society for Training & Development

Copyright 2002 Maxine Kamin   Fantastic Service Every Time

Slide 8-2

Customer Perceptions

What customers *want*

↑

compared with

↓

What customers *get*

=

Opinion of Service Quality

Copyright 2002 Maxine Kamin   Fantastic Service Every Time

Slide 8-3

Service Levels

- **Desired Service** — What you want is what you get

- **Accepted Service** — What you get is what you'll take

- **Rejected Service** — What you have is a complaint

- **Fantastic Service** — What you get is really great!

Copyright 2002 Maxine Kamin   Fantastic Service Every Time

Slide 8-4

Fantastic Service

- Amazing
- Astonishing
- Astounding
- Remarkable
- Extraordinary
- Wonderful

Miraculous

Copyright 2002 Maxine Kamin   Fantastic Service Every Time

Slide 8-5

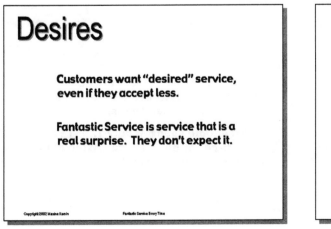

Desires

Customers want "desired" service, even if they accept less.

Fantastic Service is service that is a real surprise. They don't expect it.

Copyright 2002 Maxine Kamin   Fantastic Service Every Time

Slide 8-6

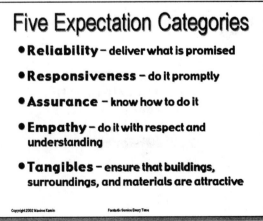

Five Expectation Categories

- **Reliability** – deliver what is promised

- **Responsiveness** – do it promptly

- **Assurance** – know how to do it

- **Empathy** – do it with respect and understanding

- **Tangibles** – ensure that buildings, surroundings, and materials are attractive

Copyright 2002 Maxine Kamin   Fantastic Service Every Time

Slide 8–7

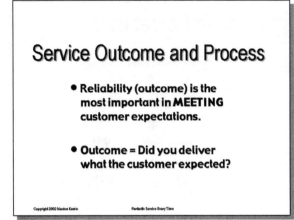

Service Outcome and Process

- Reliability (outcome) is the most important in MEETING customer expectations.

- Outcome = Did you deliver what the customer expected?

Copyright 2002 Maxine Kamin   Fantastic Service Every Time

Slide 8–8

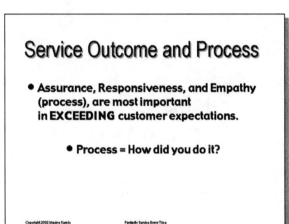

Service Outcome and Process

- Assurance, Responsiveness, and Empathy (process), are most important in EXCEEDING customer expectations.

  - Process = How did you do it?

Copyright 2002 Maxine Kamin   Fantastic Service Every Time

Slide 8–9

Fantastic Service Equation

Greeting the Customer +
Determining Needs +
Meeting Needs +
Making the Moment Memorable +
Checking Results +
Leaving the Door Open +

= Fantastic Service

Copyright 2002 Maxine Kamin   Fantastic Service Every Time

Slide 8–10

Determining
Customer Needs
Requires Two-Way
Communication

Slide 8–11

Listening

Although 50%–75% of our daily communication time is spent listening, we listen at only a 25% efficiency level.

Copyright 2002 Maxine Kamin   Fantastic Service Every Time

Slide 8–12

Listening

One of the reasons we often don't listen well is because we can think faster than we can speak.

Most people speak at only 125–150 words per minute. We can listen at up to 450 words per minute.

Copyright 2002 Maxine Kamin   Fantastic Service Every Time

Slide 8–13

Demonstrate Proactive Listening

- Give your full attention.
- Project sincerity verbally and nonverbally.
- Paraphrase.
- Respond with empathy.
- Ask open–ended and closed– ended questions.

Slide 8–14

What Gets in the Way?

Slide 8–15

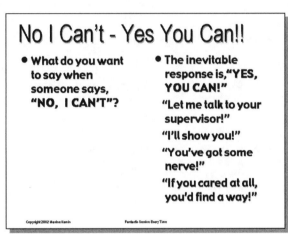

No I Can't - Yes You Can!!

- What do you want to say when someone says, "NO, I CAN'T"?

- The inevitable response is,"YES, YOU CAN!"

  "Let me talk to your supervisor!"

  "I'll show you!"

  "You've got some nerve!"

  "If you cared at all, you'd find a way!"

Slide 8–16

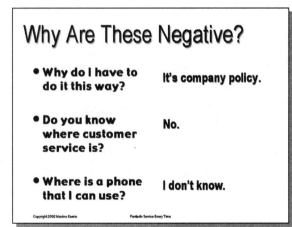

Why Are These Negative?

- Why do I have to do it this way?

  It's company policy.

- Do you know where customer service is?

  No.

- Where is a phone that I can use?

  I don't know.

Slide 8–17

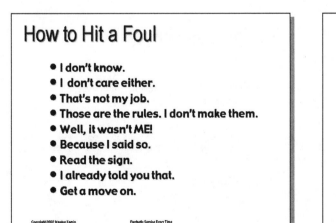

How to Hit a Foul

- I don't know.
- I don't care either.
- That's not my job.
- Those are the rules. I don't make them.
- Well, it wasn't ME!
- Because I said so.
- Read the sign.
- I already told you that.
- Get a move on.

Slide 8–18

How to Hit a Foul

Never project the following things:

- You are not welcome here.
- I do not like you.
- Your questions are stupid.
- This job bores me.
- I would rather be doing other things.

Slide 8–19

Positive Language: What Can You Do?

Negative

"You didn't fill out the paperwork properly."

Positive

"Let me help you with that part so we can get this done right away."

Fantastic Service Every Time

Slide 8–20

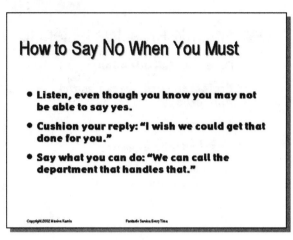

How to Say No When You Must

- Listen, even though you know you may not be able to say yes.
- Cushion your reply: "I wish we could get that done for you."
- Say what you can do: "We can call the department that handles that."

Fantastic Service Every Time

Slide 8–21

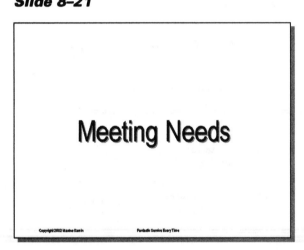

Meeting Needs

Fantastic Service Every Time

Slide 8–22

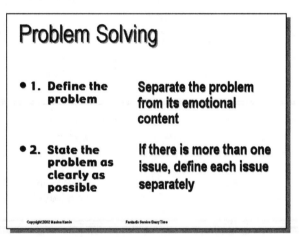

Problem Solving

- 1. Define the problem — Separate the problem from its emotional content
- 2. State the problem as clearly as possible — If there is more than one issue, define each issue separately

Fantastic Service Every Time

Slide 8–23

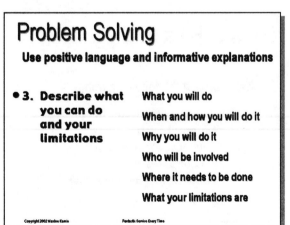

Problem Solving

Use positive language and informative explanations

- 3. Describe what you can do and your limitations
  - What you will do
  - When and how you will do it
  - Why you will do it
  - Who will be involved
  - Where it needs to be done
  - What your limitations are

Fantastic Service Every Time

Slide 8–24

Problem Solving

- 4. Agree on a solution — Provide alternatives, if appropriate
- 5. Verify the solution — Ask if the solution is acceptable and summarize agreements
- 6. Follow up — Do what you say you will do

Fantastic Service Every Time

Slide 8–25

The Final Equation Components

- **Making the Moment Memorable**
- **Checking Results**
- **Leaving the Door Open**

Copyright 2002 Maxine Kamin   Fantastic Service Every Time

Slide 8–26

Role Plays

Putting It All Together

Copyright 2002 Maxine Kamin   Fantastic Service Every Time

Slide 8–27

Be Caring and
Have Fun Out There!

**Thanks for attending
Fantastic Service Every Time**

Copyright 2002 Maxine Kamin   Fantastic Service Every Time

◆

One-Day Program

What's in This Chapter?

- ◆ Design for a one-day workshop
- ◆ Purpose and objectives of the program
- ◆ Notes on delivery and transitions
- ◆ Program agenda

This chapter provides a sample one-day training plan for Fantastic Customer Service Every Time. You may use the plan as is or you may substitute other learning activities into this design.

Chapters 1 through 5 provide background on some of the theories behind this full-day program and tips for facilitating Fantastic Customer Service training. Reading those chapters will have given you some insight into the flow of this workshop and the things you need to prepare in advance.

Customizing the content of this program will enhance your design. Within the program are many exercises that ask for examples specific to your work environment. Using actual work scenarios will make this material relevant to your own organization. There are instructions on how to expand and vary activities to extend training time for longer than one day.

The timeframe for these activities is rather tight so you may choose to skip some activities or content. Participants are likely to have many "A-ha!" experiences that naturally cover some of the content. The schedule was prepared using an 8:00 a.m. to 4:30 p.m. timeframe, which is common for organizations.

Be sure to do the role plays because they are critical to the learning process in this design.

Training Objectives

Understanding Customer Expectations:

- ◆ Determine underlying expectations of internal customers.

- ◆ Recognize levels of service.

- ◆ Identify common customer expectations.

- ◆ Describe "moments of truth."

Delivering Fantastic Service:

- ◆ Identify behaviors that constitute fantastic service.

- ◆ Practice effective listening skills.

- ◆ Use positive language.

- ◆ Practice problem solving.

- ◆ Demonstrate the Fantastic Service Equation.

Materials

For the instructor:

- ◆ This chapter for reference notes

- ◆ Learning Activity 13–1: Skills Analysis

- ◆ Learning Activity 13–2: Just Fantastic

- ◆ Learning Activity 13–3: Customer Expectations

- ◆ Learning Activity 13–4: Benefits

- ◆ Learning Activity 13–5: Governing Forces

- ◆ Learning Activity 13–6: Moments of Truth

- ◆ Learning Activity 13–7: Fantastic Service Equation

- ◆ Learning Activity 13–8: Greeting Group

- ◆ Learning Activity 13–9: Determining Needs: Communication

- ◆ Learning Activity 13–10: Noise

- Learning Activity 13–11: Body Language

- Learning Activity 13–12: Positive Language

- Learning Activity 13–13: Dealing with Anger

- Learning Activity 13–14: Meeting Needs: Problem Solving

- Learning Activity 13–15: The Final Equation Components

- Learning Activity 13–16: Putting It All Together: Role Playing

- Learning Activity 13–17: Customer Service Action Plans

- PowerPoint presentation: One-Day. To access slides for this program, open the file *One-Day.ppt* on the accompanying CD. Copies of the slides for this training session are included at the end of this chapter.

For the participants:

- Handout 13–1: Categories of Customer Expectations

- Handout 13–2: Benefits

- Handout 13–3: Governing Forces in Customer Service

- Handout 13–4: Worst Experience

- Handout 13–5: The Fantastic Service Equation

- Handout 13–6: Listening

- Handout 13–7: Paraphrase the Thought, Validate the Heart

- Handout 13–8: Positive Language

- Handout 13–9: Dealing with Anger

- Handout 13–10: Problem Solving

- Handout 13–11: Final Equation Components

- Handout 13–12: Role Plays

- Handout 13–13: Fantastic Service Equation Observation Form

- Handout 13–14: Customer Service Action Plans

- Assessment 12–1: Customer Expectations

- Assessment 12–2: Noise Detector

- Assessment 12–4: Secret Shopper

- Any prizes you want to give out (optional)

- Food (optional)

Using the CD

Materials for this training session are provided in this workbook and as electronic files on the accompanying CD. To access the electronic files, insert the CD and click on the appropriate Adobe .pdf document. Further directions and help locating and using the files can be found in the appendix, "Using the Compact Disc."

One-Day Sample Agenda: Fantastic Service Every Time

The times assigned to the elements of this training are approximate and will vary with discussion and trainer emphasis.

8:00 a.m. Welcome (5 minutes)

Welcome participants to the program, introduce yourself, and provide background about why this program is being offered and what the sponsoring organization hopes to accomplish. Let participants know that they will introduce themselves soon.

8:05 Learning Activity 13–1: Skills Analysis (chapter 13, page 107) (10 minutes)

This icebreaker gets people involved immediately. It is a fun way to introduce the customer service skills you will be addressing.

8:15 Roles and Responsibilities (5 minutes)

Describe your role and participant roles for the workshop (you might write them on a flipchart and briefly go over them). Encourage everyone to practice positive intent, keep an open mind, and think about how the concepts they will be learning might apply back at work.

8:20   Review Objectives (5 minutes)

Write the objectives of this training on a flipchart. Ask participants what they would like to get out of the session (even if they did not come to training voluntarily).

8:25   Learning Activity 13–2: Just Fantastic (chapter 13, page 110) (35 minutes)

Have participants identify their wish lists as internal customers by creating their ideal environment together in teams. Complete introductions as indicated in the instructions.

9:00   Learning Activity 13–3: Customer Expectations (chapter 13, page 114) (50 minutes)

Just like internal customers, external customers have desired expectations. Have participants complete an assessment of their perceptions of external customer expectations and discuss key expectation categories.

9:50   Learning Activity 13–4: Benefits (chapter 13, page 120) (5 minutes)

Brainstorm benefits to participants and the organization of providing excellent customer service.

9:55   Learning Activity 13–5: Governing Forces (option 1) (chapter 13, page 122) (5 minutes)

Briefly review the forces that govern customer service. See the activity for details if you would like to extend the discussion of forces.

10:00   Break (15 minutes)

10:15   Learning Activity 13–6: Moments of Truth (chapter 13, page 129) (20 minutes)

Even if all of the forces are with you, there will be times when customers are not pleased. Have participants examine their own customer service "moments of truth" to learn how to recover from organizational mishaps that cause customer dissatisfaction.

10:35   Learning Activity 13–7: Fantastic Service Equation (chapter 13, page 134) (10 minutes)

Review the equation that forms the foundation for the rest of the session.

10:45   Learning Activity 13–8: Greeting Group (chapter 13, page 137) (5 minutes)

Have participants greet each other and experience the first part of the Fantastic Service Equation.

10:50   Learning Activity 13–9: Determining Needs: Communication (chapter 13, page 139) (45 minutes)

Communication forms the basis of all customer service interactions. With mini-lectures and activities, review principles that help improve interactions with customers.

Assessment 12–4: Secret Shopper (chapter 12, page 103, or open the file *Assessment 12–4.pdf* on the CD)

Distribute this assessment for participants to complete at lunch. If they are not going to be in the building to observe your own organization, they could observe wait staff at lunch or other service providers they see.

11:35   Learning Activity 13–10: Noise (chapter 12, page 147) (25 minutes)

Listening is the cornerstone of communication. When "noise" gets in the way, it can be difficult to listen and serve customers effectively. This activity enables participants to explore noise through discussion and an assessment.

Noon   Lunch (60 minutes)

1:00   Learning Activity 13–11: Body Language (chapter 13, page 150) (10 minutes)

Explore how body language can get in the way of positive communication, and can make or break interactions with customers.

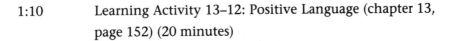

1:10   Learning Activity 13–12: Positive Language (chapter 13, page 152) (20 minutes)

Stress the importance of using positive language in the communication process to focus on what you *can* do instead of what you *can't* do.

1:30   Learning Activity 13–13: Dealing with Anger (chapter 13, page 158) (10 minutes)

Recognize that, even with a can-do attitude, dealing with angry customers requires special attention. Discuss the guidelines for dealing with difficult customers.

1:40   Learning Activity 13–14: Meeting Needs: Problem Solving (chapter 13, page 161) (20 minutes)

Review guidelines for problem solving, using a participant example to work through the steps.

2:00   Learning Activity 13–15: Final Equation Components (chapter 13, page 163) (10 minutes)

Cover the final components of the Fantastic Service Equation.

2:10   Learning Activity 13–16: Putting It All Together: Role Playing (chapter 13, page 166) (30 minutes)

Help participants develop role-play scenarios that will put together everything they have learned in the session. Role playing reinforces new behaviors—participants often say this is one of the most valuable components of the program.

2:40   Break (15 minutes)

2:55   Continue with Learning Activity 13–16: Putting It All Together (60 minutes)

Continue the role playing. This activity allows participants to practice all of the behaviors you hope to reinforce. Role plays of common work conflicts can be performed in front of the group while other participants evaluate the Fantastic Service Equation behaviors that players exhibit.

3:55   Learning Activity 13–17: Customer Service Action Plans (chapter 13, page 171) (15 minutes)

Assist participants in developing action plans that they can take back to work so they may continue to develop the skills learned in training.

4:10   Conclusion (15 minutes)

Ask what insights participants have learned through the training. Stress that your goals were to raise awareness, reinforce some of the fantastic service they are already giving, and provide new tips on how to give fantastic service every time through a systematic approach, using the Fantastic Service Equation.

4:25   Evaluation (5 minutes)

Thank the class for coming to the training and for their active participation in the program. If you learned something yourself, as trainers always do, share your insights and again thank the class for providing their expertise and experience. Give them a round of applause. If you are using an evaluation form, distribute the evaluation sheets. Tell them that they can leave the sheets at a place you designate in the room before they leave.

4:30   Close

What to Do Next

- ◆ Prepare for the one-day session.

- ◆ Compile the learning activities, assessments, handouts, and slides you will use in your training.

- ◆ Determine the schedule for training classes.

◆◆◆

The next chapter will give you some suggestions about how to provide training for leaders in your organization.

Slide 9-1

Welcome to

Fantastic Service Every Time

Maxine Kamin, M.Ed.
American Society for Training & Development

Copyright 2002 Maxine Kamin   Fantastic Service Every Time

Slide 9-2

Internal Customer Expectations

Copyright 2002 Maxine Kamin   Fantastic Service Every Time

Slide 9-3

Just Fantastic!

- People
- Customers
- Management
- Offices
- Dress Code
- Recognition
- Benefits

Copyright 2002 Maxine Kamin   Fantastic Service Every Time

Slide 9-4

Customer Perceptions

What customers *want*

⬆

compared with

⬇

What customers *get*

=

Opinion of Service Quality

Copyright 2002 Maxine Kamin   Fantastic Service Every Time

Slide 9-5

Service Levels

- Desired Service — What you want is what you get
- Accepted Service — What you get is what you'll take
- Rejected Service — What you have is a complaint
- Fantastic Service — What you get is really great!

Copyright 2002 Maxine Kamin   Fantastic Service Every Time

Slide 9-6

Fantastic Service

- Amazing
- Astonishing
- Astounding
- Remarkable
- Extraordinary
- Wonderful

Miraculous

Copyright 2002 Maxine Kamin   Fantastic Service Every Time

Slide 9–7

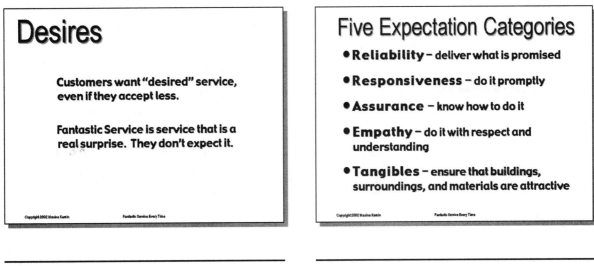

Desires

Customers want "desired" service, even if they accept less.

Fantastic Service is service that is a real surprise. They don't expect it.

Copyright 2002 Maxine Kamin   Fantastic Service Every Time

Slide 9–8

Five Expectation Categories

- **Reliability** – deliver what is promised
- **Responsiveness** – do it promptly
- **Assurance** – know how to do it
- **Empathy** – do it with respect and understanding
- **Tangibles** – ensure that buildings, surroundings, and materials are attractive

Copyright 2002 Maxine Kamin   Fantastic Service Every Time

Slide 9–9

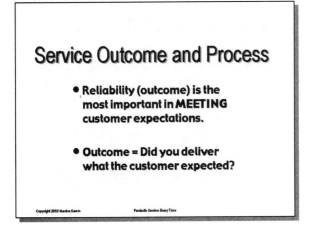

Service Outcome and Process

- Reliability (outcome) is the most important in MEETING customer expectations.

- Outcome = Did you deliver what the customer expected?

Copyright 2002 Maxine Kamin   Fantastic Service Every Time

Slide 9–10

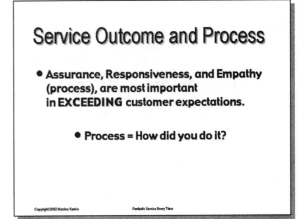

Service Outcome and Process

- Assurance, Responsiveness, and Empathy (process), are most important in EXCEEDING customer expectations.

  - Process = How did you do it?

Copyright 2002 Maxine Kamin   Fantastic Service Every Time

Slide 9–11

Benefits!

Copyright 2002 Maxine Kamin   Fantastic Service Every Time

Slide 9–12

Satisfying the Customer

YOU WILL BE:

- Helping retain jobs – yours and others
- Helping yourself by learning new skills that will be important for your continued professional growth
- Increasing your confidence
- Effectively solving customer problems
- Receiving more recognition from staff and customers
- Having more fun!

Copyright 2002 Maxine Kamin   Fantastic Service Every Time

Slide 9–13

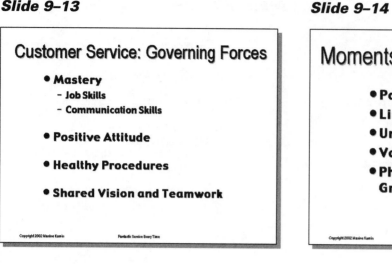

Customer Service: Governing Forces

- **Mastery**
  - Job Skills
  - Communication Skills
- **Positive Attitude**
- **Healthy Procedures**
- **Shared Vision and Teamwork**

Slide 9–14

Moments of Truth

- **Parking**
- **Lines**
- **Unexpected Fees**
- **Voice Mail**
- **Phone and Face-to-Face Greetings**

Slide 9–15

Your Worst Customer Service Experience...

Slide 9–16

Caring Is the Greatest Gift

In these days of fast companies, desktop overload, and "press 1" for service, we are all looking for a little comfort — an act of kindness to get us through the day. Caring is the greatest gift we can give someone.

It is immeasurable.

Slide 9–17

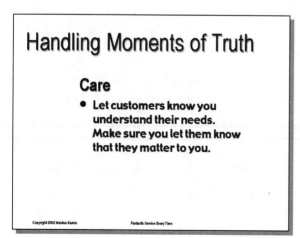

Handling Moments of Truth

Care
- Let customers know you understand their needs. Make sure you let them know that they matter to you.

Slide 9–18

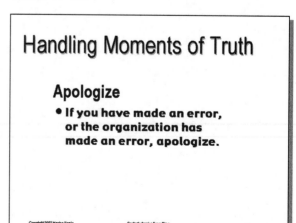

Handling Moments of Truth

Apologize
- If you have made an error, or the organization has made an error, apologize.

Slide 9–19

Handling Moments of Truth

Fix It

- Go out of your way to solve the problem. Use your own good judgment. Take the time to do what you are empowered to do to correct the situation.
- Contact your supervisor if higher authority is needed for best results.

Copyright 2002 Maxine Kamin   Fantastic Service Every Time

Slide 9–20

Fantastic Service Equation

Greeting the Customer +
Determining Needs +
Meeting Needs +
Making the Moment Memorable +
Checking Results +
Leaving the Door Open +

= Fantastic Service

Copyright 2002 Maxine Kamin   Fantastic Service Every Time

Slide 9–21

Determining
Customer Needs
Requires Two-Way
Communication

Slide 9–22

Listening

Although 50%–75% of our
daily communication time
is spent listening,
we listen at only a
25% efficiency level.

Copyright 2002 Maxine Kamin   Fantastic Service Every Time

Slide 9–23

Listening

One of the reasons we often don't listen well is because we can think faster than we can speak.

Most people speak at only 125–150 words per minute. We can listen at up to 450 words per minute.

Copyright 2002 Maxine Kamin   Fantastic Service Every Time

Slide 9–24

Demonstrate Proactive Listening

- Give your full attention.
- Project sincerity verbally and nonverbally.
- Paraphrase.
- Respond with empathy.
- Ask open-ended and closed-ended questions.

Copyright 2002 Maxine Kamin   Fantastic Service Every Time

Slide 9–25

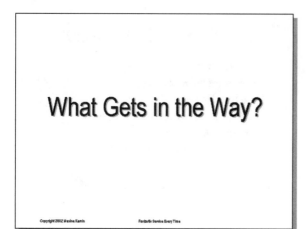

What Gets in the Way?

Copyright 2002 Maxine Kamin   Fantastic Service Every Time

Slide 9–26

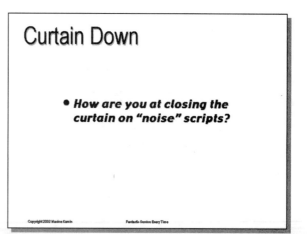

Noise

- **Filters/Values** – The script: *"You are different than I am; therefore, you're wrong."*

- **Exhaustion** – The script: *"I'm tired. I need a break. I don't want to talk to you."*

- **Mind Clutter** – The script: *"Now, what are we having for dinner tonight...oh, what was that you just said?"*

Copyright 2002 Maxine Kamin   Fantastic Service Every Time

Slide 9–27

Noise

- **Lack of Interest** – The script: *"I've heard this before...I think I'll shuffle papers while he continues...."*

- **Tone of Voice** – The script: *"She doesn't like me. She doesn't think I know what I'm doing."*

- **Evaluation/Jumping to Conclusions** – The script: *"I already know what you are going to say, so I'll make the point for you."*

Copyright 2002 Maxine Kamin   Fantastic Service Every Time

Slide 9–28

Curtain Down

- *How are you at closing the curtain on "noise" scripts?*

Copyright 2002 Maxine Kamin   Fantastic Service Every Time

Slide 9–29

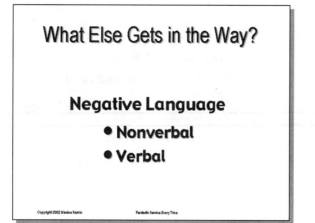

What Else Gets in the Way?

Negative Language

- Nonverbal
- Verbal

Copyright 2002 Maxine Kamin   Fantastic Service Every Time

Slide 9–30

Body Language

Is It Positive or Negative?

- Rolling eyes
- Shrugging shoulders
- Touching someone's hand
- Facing away
- Fidgeting
- Smiling

Copyright 2002 Maxine Kamin   Fantastic Service Every Time

Slide 9–31

No I Can't - Yes You Can!!

- What do you want to say when someone says, "NO, I CAN'T"?

- The inevitable response is,"YES, YOU CAN!"

  "Let me talk to your supervisor!"

  "I'll show you!"

  "You've got some nerve!"

  "If you cared at all, you'd find a way!"

Copyright 2002 Maxine Kamin   Fantastic Service Every Time

Slide 9–32

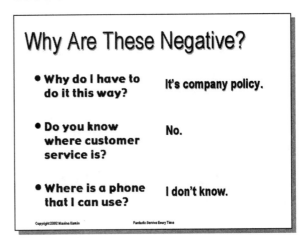

Why Are These Negative?

- Why do I have to do it this way? — It's company policy.

- Do you know where customer service is? — No.

- Where is a phone that I can use? — I don't know.

Copyright 2002 Maxine Kamin   Fantastic Service Every Time

Slide 9–33

How to Hit a Foul

- I don't know.
- I don't care either.
- That's not my job.
- Those are the rules. I don't make them.
- Well, it wasn't ME!
- Because I said so.
- Read the sign.
- I already told you that.
- Get a move on.

Copyright 2002 Maxine Kamin   Fantastic Service Every Time

Slide 9–34

How to Hit a Foul

Never project the following things:

- You are not welcome here.
- I do not like you.
- Your questions are stupid.
- This job bores me.
- I would rather be doing other things.

Copyright 2002 Maxine Kamin   Fantastic Service Every Time

Slide 9–35

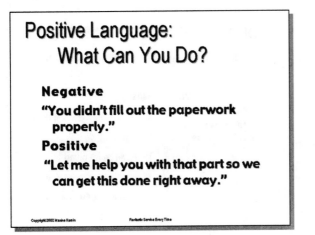

Positive Language: What Can You Do?

Negative
"You didn't fill out the paperwork properly."

Positive
"Let me help you with that part so we can get this done right away."

Copyright 2002 Maxine Kamin   Fantastic Service Every Time

Slide 9–36

How to Say No When You Must

- Listen, even though you know you may not be able to say yes.

- Cushion your reply: "I wish we could get that done for you."

- Say what you can do: "We can call the department that handles that."

Copyright 2002 Maxine Kamin   Fantastic Service Every Time

Slide 9–37

Stages of Frustration

People feel helpless.

They feel restrained.

They are ANGRY.

Slide 9–38

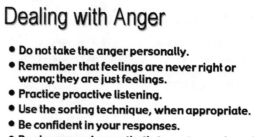

Dealing with Anger

- Do not take the anger personally.
- Remember that feelings are never right or wrong; they are just feelings.
- Practice proactive listening.
- Use the sorting technique, when appropriate.
- Be confident in your responses.
- Be sincere and empathetic to customers' needs.
- Validate feelings.
- Get the problem resolved.

Slide 9–39

Positive Language

- It would help me if...
- I do not appreciate being...
- Time out! I want to hear what you are saying, but I have to ask you to slow down a bit.
- We can talk about this. You go first and I will not interrupt you. Then when you are done, I will see if I have any questions.

Slide 9–40

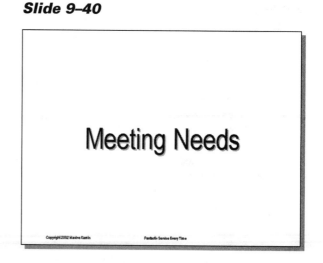

Meeting Needs

Slide 9–41

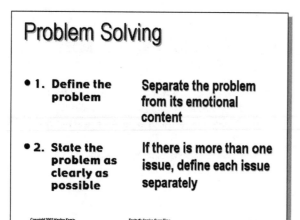

Problem Solving

- 1. Define the problem — Separate the problem from its emotional content
- 2. State the problem as clearly as possible — If there is more than one issue, define each issue separately

Slide 9–42

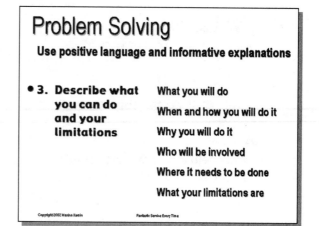

Problem Solving

Use positive language and informative explanations

- 3. Describe what you can do and your limitations
  - What you will do
  - When and how you will do it
  - Why you will do it
  - Who will be involved
  - Where it needs to be done
  - What your limitations are

Slide 9–43

Problem Solving

- **4. Agree on a solution** — Provide alternatives, if appropriate

- **5. Verify the solution** — Ask if the solution is acceptable and summarize agreements

- **6. Follow up** — Do what you say you will do

Copyright 2002 Maxine Kamin   Fantastic Service Every Time

Slide 9–44

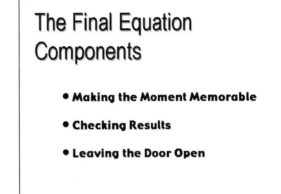

The Final Equation Components

- **Making the Moment Memorable**

- **Checking Results**

- **Leaving the Door Open**

Copyright 2002 Maxine Kamin   Fantastic Service Every Time

Slide 9–45

Role Plays

Putting It All Together

Copyright 2002 Maxine Kamin   Fantastic Service Every Time

Slide 9–46

Be Caring and Have Fun Out There!

**Thanks for attending
Fantastic Service Every Time**

Copyright 2002 Maxine Kamin   Fantastic Service Every Time

Training Executives and Supervisors

What's in This Chapter?

- Activities for organizational leaders

- How to create training for leaders

- How to use content material to create new exercises

- Handouts for leaders

This chapter provides you with ideas for training leaders in your organization. You can use these suggestions to form a two-day program that incorporates learning activities included in chapters 13 and 14. Or you may run short workshops with any combination of discussion, planning, and training that will help gain support for improving customer service in your organization.

Leadership Initiatives

Training leaders is an important part of a customer service initiative. Leadership training can help set the tone for creating organizational support for training at all levels. Chapter 3 included a series of questions for executives that you can incorporate into your training program. In addition, you might use the following steps when working with leaders:

- Meet with the executive team to solidify support for the program.

- Determine if you will use any of the methods described in chapter 3 to assess organizational need.

- Follow up in writing to confirm the steps you collectively decide to take regarding the development of the customer service initiative.

RATIONALE

Review chapters 1 and 11 regarding the bottom-line benefits of good customer service and the costs associated with losing a customer. With your leadership staff, calculate your own figures for the cost of losing a customer.

STRATEGIC PLANNING

Strategic planning is a process that involves many individuals in an organization. It is a comprehensive task. It may be beneficial to do a strategic plan as part of training for higher level leaders. One method of strategic planning is to use the questions in chapter 2 for brainstorming, and then develop a SWOT analysis of your organization, focusing on the following elements:

- ♦ **Strengths:** internal, such as commitment and infrastructure

- ♦ **Weaknesses:** internal, such as budget, time, or staff resistance

- ♦ **Opportunities:** external, such as availability of well-trained people

- ♦ **Threats:** external, such as competition or the economy.

You can generate information in several ways:

1. Create four teams to address each component. Give teams time in a training session to address one component, then repeat the brainstorming in segments for the next three components.

2. Give each team questions from chapter 3 and direct them to put the answers into the SWOT categories.

3. Divide participants into four teams. Have each team consider only one component and report back to the class. Take notes on a flipchart and add any suggestions the rest of the class would like to make.

After generating a SWOT analysis, take time to create action plans to address the issues. For more information on strategic planning, *The Balanced Scorecard* (Kaplan and Norton, 1996) is an excellent reference.

Trainings for Leaders

FANTASTIC SERVICE EVERY TIME

To promote familiarity with the program you intend to run for staff, piloting any of the activities included in this workbook will accomplish the following three goals:

1. Leaders will benefit from the training. Many executives need to practice the same skills that frontline employees need. If you describe the training as an opportunity for them to see what you will be doing with frontline workers, leaders are less likely to think, "I already know this." They also will be better able to reinforce the concepts with their employees back at work, and to set clear standards for behaviors they expect to be met.

2. Leaders are more likely to buy into the concepts you will be presenting to staff. If you introduce the Fantastic Service Equation to leaders, they can use it as a model for promoting excellence and improvement in their own departments. For example, they could use the equation in staff meetings, collect employee stories about memorable moments, and post letters of commendation from customers.

3. You will learn what leaders believe to be the most important customer service issues in their organization. Interactions with leaders will help you prepare for training other workers, and help you create relevant role plays or scenarios customized to address a particular work environment.

TIPS FOR TRAINERS

◆ Get consensus on how leaders would like procedural issues to be handled by having a whole-group discussion, or by putting people in teams to address each issue and then present their conclusions. If there are discrepancies, it may mean that more work needs to be done on procedures and empowerment issues. If this is the case, you may want to ask them to review the issues together at another time and get back to you with their recommendations.

◆ Have them construct negative and positive role plays based on the Fantastic Service Equation. You can use Handout 13–12: Role Plays

(chapter 13, page 168, or open the file *Handout 13–12.pdf* on the CD) with groups of supervisors as well as frontline workers.

◆ Use Handout 14–3: The Jones Window (chapter 14, page 179, or open the file *Handout 14–3.pdf* on the CD) to work through specific scenarios that occur at work and to develop situations to be used in training sessions.

OTHER TRAINING RECOMMENDATIONS

Use the Fantastic Service Equation to determine how executives practice internal customer service. For instance, you might ask the following questions or use the questions to create a customer service questionnaire for leaders.

Greeting:

1. How do you greet your staff members?

2. Do you make a conscious effort to say "hello"?

Determining needs:

1. How do you determine the needs of staff members?

2. How well do you listen to people when they approach you for assistance or make a suggestion?

Meeting needs:

1. How do you meet the needs of staff members?

2. How do you follow up after their requests?

3. How do you implement their suggestions?

Making the moment memorable:

1. How do you show support, encouragement, and genuine caring for staff?

2. How do you praise staff for a job well done?

3. How do you celebrate accomplishments?

Checking results:

1. How do you know if your leadership is having a positive impact on individual employees and the group?

2. How do you get feedback?

3. How do you know if employees think that you are using their suggestions?

4. What results have been accomplished as a result of the empowerment of employees?

5. How do you commend people for taking initiative?

6. How do you give feedback?

Leaving the door open:

1. Do you have an open door policy (literally)?

2. Do you make yourself available to staff? Do you have staff meetings?

3. Do staff members always know where you are?

4. Can they get in touch with you when they need you?

Show the PowerPoint slide "Five Expectation Categories" (slide 8–6) and have five teams discuss each category. Each team can describe what the organization is doing well in that category and what needs to be improved. Teams also can develop action plans for improvement.

Leadership and Customer Service

You can use the handouts included on the following pages to encourage leadership involvement in customer service improvements. You might want to put executives into teams to discuss how they think the leadership team addresses the customer service leadership areas considered in Handout 10–1: Leadership and Customer Service (page 85). You also can create your own survey based on the handout.

What to Do Next

◆ Meet with management staff to get their suggestions and buy-in.

◆ Develop a plan for training management.

◆ Decide what portions of the Fantastic Service Every Time program you will use.

◆ Compile the learning activities, assessments, handouts, and Power-Point presentations you will use in your program.

◆ Complete the training design.

◆ Pilot the program.

◆ ◆ ◆

The next chapter provides helpful information on customer service research. You may use some of that information to create learning activities for leaders or frontline participants.

Handout 10–1

Leadership and Customer Service

The Forum Corporation, in its "Customer Focus Research" project (1988), identified leadership factors that set customer-focused companies apart. This research concludes that managers set the tone for the outcome of delivering excellent customer service—what we call Fantastic Service Every Time. As a leader, you are the model for your staff. The following actions can enhance the customer service climate in your environment.

Customer Service

1. Setting customer service performance goals and standards
   - Hold discussions about what putting the customer first means to you and to the organization.
   - Communicate clear goals and standards that support high-quality service.
   - Communicate what you expect your staff to do when serving customers.
   - Develop customer service goals and standards for performance reviews.

2. Providing leadership to help solve customers' problems
   - When there is a conflict between a customer and an employee, listen to both sides of the story.
   - Let the employee know that you appreciate the thought that went into his or her response.
   - Explain your decision and why you made it.
   - Decide together how a similar situation might be handled the next time it occurs.
   - Make an effort to help remove obstacles that hinder serving customers well.
   - Set a personal example of good customer service, using excellent communication skills with internal and external customers.
   - Take some time to interact with customers directly. See how you would solve problems in the kinds of situations that your staff encounters. Discuss your interactions with staff and ask them how they would have handled the circumstances.
   - Help an employee solve a problem with another staff member or by getting information from other departments.

3. Finding better ways to obtain customer loyalty
   - Ask employees who have contact with customers for information on customer needs or expectations.
   - Seek opportunities to try new ways of doing things to serve customers better.
   - Ask and consider team members' ideas about improving the quality of products and services.

4. Helping employees enhance their customer relationships
   - Give honest and direct feedback about how well team members are serving customers.

continued on next page

Handout 10–1, continued

Leadership and Customer Service

- Help employees learn from positive and negative experiences with customers.
- Be sensitive to the "contact overload" syndrome and provide ways for employees to relieve stress.
- Observe employees' skills to see if they are in the right role.

The Internal Environment

1. Using the systems approach to serve customers
   - Identify policies and procedures that interfere with serving customers well, and change them to achieve better customer satisfaction.
   - Provide the support and resources that are needed to serve customers well.
   - Use the company's market or customer research to improve service.
   - When asked, always help staff with customer problems.
   - Provide staff with the resources they need to serve customers (equipment, tools, and physical space).
   - Insist on cooperation rather than competition within the company, and model cooperative behavior.
   - Keep all staff informed about customer needs and expectations.

2. Increasing the ability to serve customers
   - Cross-train staff to maximize use of talents, keep learning interesting, and encourage people to assist other departments.
   - Encourage employees to feel that being responsive to customer needs is their personal responsibility, and not someone else's job.
   - Function as a team in serving customers.
   - Ensure that customer relations skills are an important factor in deciding who is hired to work with customers.
   - Reward employees for doing a good job of serving customers.

3. Valuing excellence
   - Resolve customers' problems to their satisfaction.
   - Personally provide high-quality service to customers.
   - Meet the goals and standards for the level of service quality the company expects.

4. Relating with customers
   - Regularly ask customers about their needs or expectations.
   - Regularly collect feedback from customers about the quality of the service received.
   - Employ a "whatever it takes" policy to remedy the situation for a dissatisfied customer or one with a special need.
   - Use information about the needs or expectations of customers to identify ways to serve them better.

Handout 10–2

Motivating Team Members

Each person on your team is unique. Motivating people with different personalities and different needs is not easy, but it can be challenging and rewarding.

It has been said that *hope is the magic ingredient to motivation.* This is a powerful statement. Hope for making things better, for succeeding, and for making a difference in an organization are powerful motivators.

> Motivation factors prompt employees to do a better job and to improve productivity. Theorists suggest that the four strongest motivation factors are
>
> 1. **Achievement:** Feeling personal accomplishment for having done a job well
>
> 2. **Recognition:** Being recognized for doing your job well; for example, being complimented by your boss or receiving an award
>
> 3. **Participation:** Being personally involved in your work; having some responsibility for making decisions
>
> 4. **Growth:** Having the opportunity for a challenge in the job, such as the chance to learn skills and knowledge.

Increasing Motivation

Achievement and recognition are strong motivators. Here are some ways that managers can help increase the harmony and productivity of staff:

◆ Recognize achievement when you see it.

◆ Recognize steps toward reaching a goal; don't always wait for the end product or total behavior change.

◆ Make up a list of ways you can show appreciation. Include some ways that would be a stretch for you—things you would not ordinarily think about doing.

◆ On a weekly basis, record at least one achievement that has been accomplished by each one of your staff members. Note whether you recognized the achievement. Then do as suggested above to notice and recognize more achievement.

Praise

When asked what type of recognition people want, the answer is often, "I just wish my boss would say 'hello.'" How often that comes up; how simple it seems. Here are a number of other ways to recognize employees:

continued on next page

Handout 10–2, continued
Motivating Team Members

- Give thank-you cards at work.

- Send thank-you cards to employees' homes.

- Present "job well done" cards.

- Tell people how good you feel about what they did and how it helps the organization.

- Take a staff member out to lunch or dinner as a reward for a specific project.

- Organize employee events and activities, or lead an employee activities committee that includes staff members.

- Give specific praise in front of others.

- Arrange for employees to have lunch or breakfast with the head of the organization.

- Give time off.

- Delegate. (This is a reward to many team members because it shows your faith and trust.)

- Work on the front line with your staff.

- Hold informative meetings about the company.

- Offer professional workshops and fun workshops.

- Frame and display positive letters from customers.

- Do a cheer with your group one morning.

- Create a company song with staff. Videotape the production.

- Take some time to walk around during the day to observe your area.

- Have informal discussions with staff during your walks.

- Have an outstanding employee spend a day with an important executive.

If you are at a loss for ideas, the book *1001 Ways to Reward Employees* by Bob Nelson (1994) is a good source of inspiration.

Chapter 11

Customer Service and the Bottom Line

- ♦ Costs of losing customers
- ♦ Customer expectations
- ♦ Other factors affecting customer relations

This chapter gives you some additional information about the importance of good customer service. You can use this material in discussion or in creating your own activities.

The Cost of Losing a Customer

The statistics in the first chapter of this workbook indicated how expensive it is to lose customers. Those statistics came from Technical Assistance Research Programs and the Forum Corporation.

TARP's research included several landmark studies, including "Consumer Complaint Handling in America," a series of reports for member agencies of the Consumer Affairs Council that were prepared at the request of the U.S. Office of Consumer Affairs (1985, 1986). Those studies have been popularized in many sources. When authors and speakers begin with the phrase, "Researchers say...," the researchers often are TARP associates. Many companies that sell motivational materials distribute plaques and posters that feature TARP's study results.

More recent ongoing research by TARP confirms the findings of the original consumer affairs study, although statistics vary by industry. Here are some updates from TARP's John Goodman (1999):

- ♦ On average, across all industries, 50 percent of consumers' complaints are presented to a frontline person. In retail and distributor industries, the chances are high that a problem never will be reported to the manufacturer or corporate office.

◆   Only one to five percent of customers bring their complaints to a manager or corporate office.

◆   For small-ticket items, only four to 20 percent of customers complain to a frontline staff member. Ninety-six percent of those customers do not complain beyond the front line.

◆   For large-ticket items, the complaint rate is higher: Up to 50 percent complain to frontline personnel and five to 10 percent take complaints to a higher level.

◆   If a company has an 800 number, the number of complaints that reach a corporate office may double in number (TARP recommends a toll-free line as a way to collect data on and resolve complaints).

◆   If a complaint is resolved quickly, or on the first contact, there is 10 percent higher satisfaction and loyalty than if a consumer has to go through many contacts for problem resolution.

◆   Customers who complain and are satisfied are up to eight percent more loyal than if they had encountered no problem at all.

◆   Approximately 20 percent of dissatisfaction is caused by employee actions, 40 percent by corporate products and processes that do not meet expectations, and up to 40 percent is the result of customer mistakes or incorrect expectations.

The hypothetical scenario presented in Figure 11–1 takes into account some of the costs of losing a customer. If you plug in your organization's numbers, this chart can be a good way to illustrate the importance of customer service training to executives. Have your management staff bring numbers and calculate the costs of losing customers as an exercise in a training program. It can be a valuable exercise (literally!) to look at the financial consequences of customer attrition.

Customer Expectations

Customer predictions, or expectations, can be positive ideals. An expectation may be the wished-for level of performance that would completely satisfy the customer. Customer expectations also can be negative, based on previous experiences that were perceived as inadequate. Those predictions might emerge from what customers think typical service looks like, or their beliefs that what is advertised usually differs from the real thing.

Expectations influence how customers view an organization or business and even how they view individual service representatives. Some customers

---

Figure 11–1
Customer Service and Lost Revenue

TARP's research shows that

- typically, 25 percent of customers are dissatisfied with service in a given business.
- among the dissatisfied, 70 percent of those whose complaints are not satisfactorily resolved will not continue doing business with that organization.
- each dissatisfied person will tell 10 other people about a negative experience.
- of those told, 2 percent (one in 50) will not purchase services from that organization.

Imagine a business with a total annual revenue of $10,000,000 and 2,500 customers (an average revenue of $4,000 per customer).

With poor customer service, they create 625 dissatisfied customers (25 percent of 2,500).

If 70 percent of those customers do not return, the organization loses 437.5 customers (70 percent of 625), or $1,750,000 in revenue (437.5 × $4,000).

If the dissatisfied customers each tell 10 people (625 × 10), that's 6,250 who receive the negative word of mouth, and 125 of them (2 percent of 6,250) will not buy services in the future.

At $4,000 per customer, that's an additional potential revenue loss of $500,000.

In this example, the total annual revenue lost because of poor customer service is $1,750,000 + $500,000, or $2,250,000, or 22.5 percent of total revenue.

- This does not take into account the cost of replacing a customer, which is two to 20 times what it costs to keep one.
- This also does not take into account each customer's lifetime value. If satisfied with services, a customer's lifetime with an organization averages 10 years, so potential loss per unhappy customer is up to 10 times the loss projected here.

Note that if half of the dissatisfied customers returned, the revenue impact would be greater than $1,000,000, and the organization would avoid the costs of acquiring that many brand-new customers!

believe they cannot get the service they want from regular channels in an organization, but they find they can get good service from certain representatives. They might hold on to those representatives' telephone numbers for dear life, and call whenever they have problems with the organization, because they feel they have found a person who will help find a solution.

There are customers who expect the worst. Perhaps they have had bad experiences and they expect that all transactions will be equally bad. If such a customer returns to the original organization and has a very positive experience, her wished-for needs are met, her perception improves, and if there are any memorable moments that include a special touch, she will go away with a very high level of satisfaction.

Those who expect to receive what they wish for (that is, a high level of performance) sometimes will tolerate disappointment, depending on what they perceive as the cause of the problem. If the cause appears beyond the control of the company in question (perhaps a disaster has caused a late delivery), customers may be more understanding.

Events that occur before a customer gets to the environment also may determine satisfaction levels. A customer in a very good state of mind may be more accepting of disappointments. If the customer is angry or upset, even if that anger has nothing to do with the company, he may not be as forgiving.

Personalities also enter into the picture. Some people are just more tolerant than others. But it is important to remember that people who appear tolerant because they do not complain may simply vote with their feet and go elsewhere next time.

Customers who have unrealistic expectations or demands need a lot of assurance and empathy. A customer service representative can deal effectively with unrealistic demands by using the communication techniques suggested throughout this workbook.

Len Berry and researchers at Texas A&M University have written groundbreaking work on customer expectations. Their excellent summary can be found in the article "The Nature and Determinants of Customer Expectations of Service" (1993). Berry has written a number of books that are useful reading for anyone interested in foundational research on customer service.

In addition to the work of Berry and his associates, *Delivering Knock Your Socks Off Service,* by Kristin Anderson and Ron Zemke (1998), is a good reference for examples of the five expectation categories discussed in Learning Activity 13–3: Customer Expectations.

Other Factors

GOVERNING FORCES

There are many governing forces that contribute to the delivery of excellent customer service. It takes a village, so to speak. Consistent with systems theory, the concept of governing forces indicates that all parts of an organization need to be connected to produce a desired result. Without all the governing forces on the positive side of the scale, customer service initiatives can be sabotaged by the very organizations that hope to improve their service. Change takes time and effort, and for customer service programs to work, support must be system-wide.

MOMENTS OF TRUTH

"Moment of truth" is a well-known term in the world of customer service, and a concept that has been discussed by many authors, including Karl Albrecht (1990). A moment of truth occurs when a customer comes into contact with a customer service representative or a department and makes judgments about the facilities or the service received. According to Albrecht, the term "moment of truth" comes from Spanish bullfights, where the moment when a matador and bull come face to face is referred to as *el momento de verdad.* In that moment, something must happen.

Moments of truth determine how a customer feels about an organization and its employees, and they can determine future loyalty. Unfortunately, moments of truth are not cumulative. Customers generally do not consider their many experiences with an organization. Rather, it is the last contact, good or bad, that affects their opinion.

What to Do Next

♦ Continue to review current research.

♦ Determine how customer service research might apply to your organization.

♦ Present relevant findings to your management team.

◆ Determine the potential return-on-investment for improving customer service in your organization.

◆ ◆ ◆

The next chapter includes assessments that can be used in your training programs. The assessments help participants recognize their opinions about customers and about their own skills in the customer service environment.

◆

Assessments

What's in This Chapter?

- ◆ Four assessments for eliciting trainees' perceptions
- ◆ Follow-up questions

This chapter contains assessments that you can use to gather information about participants' perceptions. You can use these assessments in conjunction with activities or construct activities around them. The instruments presented here are guides for learning, and are *not* intended to be evaluation tools.

- ◆ Assessment 12–1 helps participants identify their own opinions about customer needs.

- ◆ Assessment 12–2 is a self-assessment regarding listening skills and behaviors.

- ◆ Assessment 12–3 corresponds with the components of the Fantastic Service Equation.

- ◆ Assessment 12–4 is a simple observational check sheet.

Using the CD

The assessments presented in this chapter also appear on the accompanying CD. You will find those assessments by inserting the CD and using Adobe Acrobat software to open the .pdf file(s) for the specific assessment(s) you wish to use in your training. When you locate the file(s) you need, simply print out the pages of the document(s) for your session.

What to Do Next

◆ Review training activities to see where assessments would be useful.

◆ Consider developing other activities to augment the assessments.

◆ Include the assessments you choose in your training program.

◆◆◆

The next chapter includes the learning activities required for the three program designs that are outlined in this workbook. The learning activities can be used as suggested in the agendas included in chapters 7, 8, and 9 or as stand-alone activities.

Assessment 12–1
Customer Expectations

Instructions: Given your experience as a customer and as a customer service specialist, how important do you think the behaviors and feelings listed below are to customers? On a scale from 1 to 4, evaluate the significance of the following behaviors and feelings from the customers' perspective. Write the number on the line to the left of each item.

1 = VERY IMPORTANT   3 = SOMEWHAT IMPORTANT

2 = IMPORTANT   4 = NOT IMPORTANT

How important are the following service behaviors to customers?

_____ 1. Representatives obviously know their jobs and can answer questions in terms that customers understand.

_____ 2. Representatives deliver on organization and personal promises.

_____ 3. Representatives apologize for errors, even when the fault is not clearly theirs.

_____ 4. Representatives greet people with a smile.

_____ 5. Representatives do things quickly.

_____ 6. Representatives tell customers how long it will take to get things done.

_____ 7. Representatives give clear directions to customers.

_____ 8. Representatives allow customers to speak to "the boss" if they ask.

_____ 9. Representatives do things right the first time.

_____ 10. Representatives provide assistance even outside their areas.

From the customers' perspective, how important is it to feel the following ways in their interactions with service representatives?

_____ 11. Good about their customer service experiences

_____ 12. Important

_____ 13. Respected

_____ 14. Special

_____ 15. Appreciated for their business

_____ 16. Listened to and understood

_____ 17. In control of the situation

_____ 18. Valued for their suggestions

_____ 19. Physically comfortable in an appealing environment

_____ 20. As though the representative is on the customer's side.

Assessment 12–2
Noise Detector

Instructions: This assessment will help you determine the areas in which your listening skills are strong and those in which you think you can improve. For each item below, circle the number from 1 to 4 corresponding to the answer that most accurately reflects your skill level.

LISTENING BEHAVIOR	DO THIS WELL	DO THIS FAIRLY WELL	COULD IMPROVE	NEED SUBSTANTIAL IMPROVEMENT
1. I listen well to people whose accents or ethnic backgrounds differ from mine.	1	2	3	4
2. I welcome interactions with people who have values that differ from mine.	1	2	3	4
3. When I am tired, I make an extra effort to listen to others.	1	2	3	4
4. When people are shouting or being aggressive, I listen carefully to decipher their message.	1	2	3	4
5. When someone is sarcastic, I ask questions to find out what he or she is thinking.	1	2	3	4
6. I am eager to work through misunderstandings when they arise.	1	2	3	4
7. I listen to others with full attention, regardless of the topic or my level of interest in the discussion.	1	2	3	4
8. I make a conscious effort to paraphrase others' remarks.	1	2	3	4
9. I listen to everything a person has to say before I draw conclusions.	1	2	3	4
10. I let people finish their sentences.	1	2	3	4
11. When I am upset or anxious, I can put my concerns aside in order to be there for others.	1	2	3	4
12. When I am listening, I tune out all distractions.	1	2	3	4
13. I acknowledge other peoples' feelings.	1	2	3	4

continued on next page

Assessment 12–2, continued
Noise Detector

LISTENING BEHAVIOR	DO THIS WELL	DO THIS FAIRLY WELL	COULD IMPROVE	NEED SUBSTANTIAL IMPROVEMENT
14. Others know that I am interested in what they are saying by my body language.	1	2	3	4
15. I remain silent to allow others to finish talking.	1	2	3	4

Noise Detector Scoring

- How many listening behaviors did you circle at each of the four skill levels?

    Do This Well: _____

    Do This Fairly Well: _____

    Could Improve: _____

    Need Substantial Improvement: _____

- List the item numbers you rated at each of the levels.

    Do This Well: _____

    Do This Fairly Well: _____

    Could Improve: _____

    Need Substantial Improvement: _____

- In what areas would you like to improve your ability to listen effectively?

- What are some ways that you could improve in those areas?

Assessment 12–3
Fantastic Service Every Time Survey

Instructions: How often do you carry out the behaviors that result in fantastic service every time? Next to each behavior listed below, write the number from 1 to 4 that indicates how frequently you act or respond in these ways.

1 = ALMOST ALWAYS   3 = SOMETIMES
2 = MOST OF THE TIME   4 = RARELY

Greeting

_____ 1. When I come in to work I say "hello" to everyone, including those in my work unit and those I see on the way in.

_____ 2. When working with customers I make eye contact first and greet them with a smile.

_____ 3. I answer the phone with a smile.

_____ 4. When people are waiting, I acknowledge them and let them know I will be with them as soon as I can.

Total score for this section _____

Determining Needs

_____ 5. I find it easy to listen to customers, even when they are rambling.

_____ 6. I repeat or paraphrase important requests to ensure that I understand what a customer needs.

_____ 7. I am good at dealing with intense emotions at work.

_____ 8. Even if I think I know what customers want, I ask questions that help me figure out what they really need.

Total score for this section _____

Meeting Needs

_____ 9. If a customer is angry with me or has a negative attitude, I go out of my way to give that person good service.

_____ 10. I apologize for errors whether or not I was responsible for them.

_____ 11. I do things quickly.

_____ 12. I keep my word.

Total score for this section _____

Making the Moment Memorable

_____ 13. I would take time out of my schedule to walk a person where he or she needs to go, rather than just give directions.

_____ 14. If a customer has called several times, I will make a call myself to ensure that the customer reaches the right person.

continued on next page

Assessment 12–3, continued

Fantastic Service Every Time Survey

_____ **15.** I welcome the chance to help other workers solve problems for customers, even when I'm busy.

_____ **16.** I enjoy finding ways to please customers.

Total score for this section _____

Checking Results

_____ **17.** I ask customers what they think about our service.

_____ **18.** I ask if there is anything else we can do, even if the transaction is finished.

_____ **19.** I ask customers if they will come back or if they would use our services again.

_____ **20.** I ask customers for their opinions on how we can make our service even better.

Total score for this section _____

Leaving the Door Open

_____ **21.** I give my name or card to customers in case they need to contact me again.

_____ **22.** I sometimes follow up by calling a customer to see if a problem or issue was resolved.

_____ **23.** I invite customers to come back if I think they might be interested in something we have to offer.

_____ **24.** I appreciate customers for coming in and using our services.

Total score for this section _____

Assessment TOTAL _____

SURVEY RESULTS

Review each section of the survey to see if there are areas in which you would like to make improvements. Are there any sections in which "Almost Always" or "Most of the Time" is not enough? For each assessment section, list the ways you can continue to demonstrate excellent customer service skills, and the ways you can improve. Write down those ways in the spaces provided below.

Greeting

◆ Continue:

◆ Improve:

continued on next page

Assessment 12–3, continued
Fantastic Service Every Time Survey

Determining Needs

- Continue:

- Improve:

Meeting Needs

- Continue:

- Improve:

Making the Moment Memorable

- Continue:

- Improve:

Checking Results

- Continue:

- Improve:

Leaving the Door Open

- Continue:

- Improve:

Assessment 12–4
Secret Shopper

Instructions: A greeting is the first interaction a customer notices. In a customer service setting, observe whether staff members meet and greet customers. Make a checkmark in the appropriate boxes.

NAME OF STAFF MEMBER

☐ Greeting	☐ Smile
☐ Greeting	☐ Smile
☐ Greeting	☐ Smile
☐ Greeting	☐ Smile
☐ Greeting	☐ Smile
☐ Greeting	☐ Smile
☐ Greeting	☐ Smile
☐ Greeting	☐ Smile
☐ Greeting	☐ Smile
☐ Greeting	☐ Smile
☐ Greeting	☐ Smile
☐ Greeting	☐ Smile
☐ Greeting	☐ Smile
☐ Greeting	☐ Smile
☐ Greeting	☐ Smile
☐ Greeting	☐ Smile
☐ Greeting	☐ Smile
☐ Greeting	☐ Smile
☐ Greeting	☐ Smile
☐ Greeting	☐ Smile
☐ Greeting	☐ Smile

◆

Learning Activities

◆ Tips for trainers

◆ Seventeen learning activities

◆ Fourteen handouts and other materials

This chapter includes all of the learning activities that are used in the designs for the one-hour, half-day, and full-day training sessions presented in previous chapters.

Using the CD

You will find the learning activities, handouts, slides, and other materials included in this chapter on the CD that accompanies this workbook. To access these files, insert the CD and click on the following file names:

◆ *Assessment* [number].*pdf*

◆ *Handout* [number].*pdf*

◆ *One-Hour.ppt*

◆ *Half-Day.ppt*

◆ *One-Day.ppt*

To print out the materials for your training session, follow these simple steps. Insert the CD and click on the appropriate .pdf file name to open it in Adobe Acrobat software. Print out the pages of the document(s) needed for your training session.

In this chapter, the slides referred to in each of the learning activities are numbered according to the order in which they appear on the CD in the one-day program. You can access individual slides by opening the one-day PowerPoint presentation *(One-Day.ppt)*. You can choose individual slides to suit your customized content by opening the one-day presentation, saving the file under a different name, and deleting the slides you do not want to use. Thumbnails of the slides in that presentation will appear and you can copy and paste any of them into your own presentation.

For additional instructions on using the CD, see the appendix, "Using the Compact Disc," at the end of the workbook.

Tips for Trainers

Before using these learning activities in your training sessions, be sure to review chapters 1 through 4 for background on how this training program was developed. Chapter 5 included tips on facilitation, including preparation, room setup, and how to address the flow of the session.

As in all training, adding your personal touch by sharing your own stories will help make the content come alive. Feel free to describe your experiences with good and bad service whenever those examples might be helpful. Customizing the learning activities with examples from your organization (or the trainees' organization, if you are a consultant) also will add value to the program.

Be flexible. The timeframes for many of these activities can be changed according to your own goals and needs. You may find that you cover key concepts in the course of discussion and that you no longer need to include certain activities or content modules.

Learning Activity 13–1: Skills Analysis

GOALS

The goals of this activity are

- ◆ to create a spirit of cooperation

- ◆ to introduce the customer service skills of listening, communicating, giving directions, and teamwork

- ◆ to energize participants as an icebreaker.

MATERIALS

The materials needed for this activity are

- ◆ watch with a second hand

- ◆ space large enough for people to line up (classroom or hallway).

TIME

- ◆ 10 minutes

INSTRUCTIONS

Begin with the following introductory remarks:

"To take a baseline of your current customer service skills, I am going to measure the extent to which you already have some of the most important customer service competencies. These skills include the ability to

- ◆ *listen*

- ◆ *communicate*

- ◆ *give directions and*

- ◆ *demonstrate teamwork.*

"We will be timing this exercise to see how quickly you can reach your goal. In any customer service environment, it is important not only to deliver good service and accomplish the tasks at hand—it is also important to provide service quickly and efficiently."

Ask if customers sometimes expect "instant service." You should get a few nods and laughs. Move right into the rest of the directions after you receive and reinforce participants' responses. Ask someone with a second hand on his or her watch to be the timekeeper and observer of the exercise.

Say, *"I am now going to give you directions for this assignment. You need to listen carefully."* Then give the following instructions: *"I want you to line up in order of your birth date.* Participants probably will laugh, thinking about who is the oldest, although they soon will see that age is not relevant in this exercise.

Say, *"Line up in order of the month and day, not the year. We will be timing you. When I say 'five, four, three, two, one,' you may begin."*

Look at your watch. Explain that they must tell you when they are through with the exercise, and that you will ask the timekeeper to call time when they give you a signal. If they are confused about the exercise, *do not do anything;* just repeat the original directions. If they ask where the line should start, reply, *"It's up to you."*

Count down and let them line up.

When they give you the signal that they are finished, ask the timekeeper how many seconds they took. Ask for a round of applause. Compliment the group for completing the line quickly.

Tell them that you now are going to check for quality. Start at the January end of the line and ask each person to give his or her birth date. Repeat each date with enthusiasm after the person has said it. Give a final round of applause for efficiency (the number of seconds it took) and 100 percent quality (or the number of seconds and *almost* 100 percent quality, whatever the case might be).

DEBRIEFING

Thank participants for doing the exercise. While they are still standing, ask, *"What did you notice about how you went about the activity?"* You also might ask some of the following specific questions:

1. Who gave directions?

2. Who helped others?

3. How well did you listen to each other?

4. How well did you communicate?

5. How well did you work toward a goal and demonstrate teamwork?

KEY POINTS

Point out that all of the skills they used are skills necessary for good customer service, and that they were able to demonstrate the essentials. Tell them that they passed the test. (You might want to highlight some skills that you saw them demonstrate.)

Tell them that throughout the session they will be sharing skills with each other and learning new techniques to use in difficult situations or when they find it hard to draw on the skills they have. Give them another round of applause and let them go back to their seats.

Learning Activity 13–2: Just Fantastic

GOALS

The goals of this activity are

- ◆ to introduce participants to each other
- ◆ to determine expectations of internal customers
- ◆ to create an atmosphere of openness and trust
- ◆ to identify common internal customer expectations.

MATERIALS

The materials needed for this activity are

- ◆ flipchart with full pad of paper
- ◆ two colors of marking pens per team
- ◆ magazines, scissors (optional)
- ◆ masking tape
- ◆ PowerPoint slides: "Internal Customer Expectations" (slide 2), "Just Fantastic!" (slide 3).

TIME

- ◆ 35 minutes

INSTRUCTIONS

Explain that all customers, external and internal, have expectations and ideas about how an organization should deliver services. Tell participants that in this activity they will be considering what they would see in their organization if it were working at its optimum level.

Show the "Internal Customer Expectations" slide. Tell participants that they will be creating a model for their own organization based on what they (internal customers—those who provide services to each other) would like to see. Explain that they will be creating a drawing of what their organization looks like and does, and listing key concepts as well. (Or you might have them create collages using magazine pictures to depict their optimum organization.)

Tell participants that their pictures and descriptions may address anything that is important to them, such as

- what staff members are like

- how they treat each other

- how they treat customers

- what customers are like

- what the offices and buildings look like

- what the dress code is

- what the characteristics of managers and supervisors are

- how people get paid and rewarded

- how policies and procedures are created and implemented.

Show the "Just Fantastic!" slide. Tell participants that some sample categories of what they might include in their drawings and collages are listed on the slide (for example, people, facilities) but that they may include anything they want.

Explain that they should make drawings or pictures on the left side of the flipchart paper and write words on the right side. They can use three-quarters of the page for representations and one-quarter for words.

Divide the class into teams of seven or eight (or at least three teams). Give each team a piece of flipchart paper and at least two marking pens (or magazines, tape, and scissors if collages are planned).

When teams have formed, repeat the directions. Then tell each group to choose a leader who will present their "fantastic" organization at the completion of the exercise. Circulate among the groups to help them get started. Encourage them to be creative.

After 15 minutes, let the groups know that they have five more minutes. Five minutes later, check to see that everyone is finished. If a group is not finished, give two more minutes and coach them to complete the project.

Ask for the first volunteer leader to present a finished product. Tape the first group's flipchart paper to a wall. Have the leader stand next to the paper and describe the group's work.

After each presentation, ask every person in the group to introduce himself or herself. On your flipchart write the following information that should be included in the introductions:

- name

- one word that describes what would be most important to you in your optimum organization

- unit in which you work

- number of years you have been with the organization.

Continue until all groups are finished. Remember that applause can energize the group after everyone has presented or whenever they need a lift.

Variation

You may vary this activity in the following way:

- Give each participant index cards, small pieces of paper (you can cut up and recycle any kind of paper), or Post-it notes. Have each person write one essential aspect that characterizes a fantastic organization on a card.

- Have them share cards.

- Tell the group to cluster the cards into categories (people, environment, policies).

- Ask them to post the cards in categories on a flipchart sheet.

- Discuss.

DEBRIEFING

Begin by saying, *"As internal customers, you all have ideal expectations. You may differ on what you want most, but you would like certain standards to be met, even in your work as it exists today."*

Then ask the following questions:

1. What common expectations are evident in your drawings?

2. What themes came up repeatedly?

3. What did you notice about the concepts people chose to describe a fantastic organization?

4.   What would you be willing to give up if you had to?

5.   What would you not be willing to give up?

6.   How would you feel if you had to give some items up?

It also will be helpful to ask these questions about the group process:

1.   What did you notice about how your group interacted in this exercise?

2.   Was there a leader?

3.   Was everyone included?

4.   Who did what, and why?

5.   Did you all feel good about the product and process?

KEY POINTS

Point out that the satisfaction of internal customers regarding what you do (the task and outcome) and how you do it (your process) is the basis of good service for both internal and external customers.

Learning Activity 13–3: Customer Expectations

GOALS

The goals of this activity are

- ◆ to emphasize the importance of customer expectations

- ◆ to recognize how expectations are formed

- ◆ to define categories of expectations.

MATERIALS

The materials needed for this activity are

- ◆ PowerPoint slides: "Customer Perceptions" (slide 4), "Service Levels" (slide 5), "Fantastic Service" (slide 6), "Desires" (slide 7), "Five Expectation Categories" (slide 8), "Service Outcome and Process" (slides 9 and 10)

- ◆ Assessment 12–1: Customer Expectations

- ◆ Handout 13–1: Categories of Customer Expectations

- ◆ flipchart and marking pen.

TIME

- ◆ 35 minutes, or 50 minutes with additional exercise

INSTRUCTIONS

Explain that this is an exercise that focuses on specific external customer expectations.

Show the "Customer Perceptions" slide.

Explain, *"Usually customers come in with preconceived notions or predictions about what service will be like. Whether those expectations are fulfilled influences how they perceive the quality of service delivered, whether they will come back, and whether they will speak favorably or unfavorably to others about the organization. This all translates into dollars."*

Show the "Service Levels" slide. Ask the following questions:

1. What kind of word-of-mouth advertising would you expect in each of the four levels?

2. What consequence would word-of-mouth have on the organization?

Show the "Fantastic Service" and "Desires" slides. Explain that in this program participants will be working to provide fantastic service.

Distribute Assessment 12–1: Customer Expectations. Explain that the assessment should reflect participants' views of external customers' desired expectations.

Give the class five minutes to fill out the assessment. When everyone is done, ask what people thought were some of the most important expectations. Ask how many chose "Not Important" for any items. If there are no "Not Important" answers, ask how many chose "Somewhat Important" for any items.

Discuss the items that people checked as "Not Important" (or "Somewhat Important"). Ask about the reasoning behind considering those issues to be less important. Although all of the items on the assessment represent real customer expectations, participants may have viable reasons for thinking that some are less significant. You do not need to discuss every question in detail because there will be consensus on many answers.

Variation

You may vary this activity in the following ways:

♦   Conduct this assessment by putting the class into groups, pairs, or trios to discuss answers.

♦   Use the assessment to generate a list of questions that participants would like to address in the training session. Write this list on a flipchart and keep it to refer to later in the program (this is a "parking lot" list).

KEY POINTS FOR THE ASSESSMENT

When specific items on the assessment do come up in discussion, highlight the following points:

1. **Representatives obviously know their jobs and can answer questions in terms that customers understand.** Customers don't like to be talked down to, and they don't like to hear jargon or language specific to the organization. Even if staff members are new,

customers still think they should know their jobs or have backup to go to for answers.

2. **Representatives deliver on organization and personal promises.** Organizations make promises via advertising, mission statements, and procedures. Employees often make promises to call back or to have an item ready in the future. Customers expect the organization and its representatives to fulfill promises.

3. **Representatives apologize for errors, even when the fault is not clearly theirs.** An apology can be "I'm so sorry that you were inconvenienced." It doesn't have to assume blame.

4. **Representatives greet people with a smile.** This is key and will be covered in depth later.

5. **Representatives do things quickly.** Customers don't like it when someone takes his own sweet time doing something. They expect efficiency and quality.

6. **Representatives tell customers how long it will take to get things done.** It's important to be honest about how long it will take to accomplish something. Giving accurate timeframes enables customers to decide whether they can wait and prevents frustration and repeated call-backs.

7. **Representatives give clear directions to customers.** People need very specific directions regarding how to get somewhere, how to fill out forms, when items are due, what documents they need, and why they need them.

8. **Representatives allow customers to speak to "the boss," if they ask.** It is best to handle problems at the frontline level, but this is not always possible. It is important not to argue with a customer if he or she wants to speak to someone higher up, and it is good to discuss these policies as a work team to be sure that there are ways to handle escalated situations comfortably. Sometimes another customer service representative or team leader can step in to handle a situation.

9. **Representatives do things right the first time.** Doing things right saves time and establishes credibility.

10. **Representatives provide assistance even outside their areas.** Customers don't care whose job it is. They expect you to help solve

their problem, even if you have to call another department or contact another person to assist you.

REGARDING FEELINGS

People just want to feel good when they are in a service situation. Most people have plenty of problems, issues, and annoyances at work and at home. When they need service, they have psychological expectations of acceptance and appreciation. They also expect neat, clean, and attractive surroundings.

Good listening includes giving a customer your full attention and working to understand his or her real message. It is important to validate customer input—they often have valuable suggestions.

Although customers probably know that they are not in control of the situation, they sometimes want to be. They want what they want, and they want it now. Sometimes they also want to tell people how to do things. It is very hard for some people not to give orders.

Show the "Five Expectation Categories" slide and discuss the categories. Show the "Service Outcome and Process" slides.

KEY POINTS

Summarize the five categories of customer expectations. Remind participants that service representatives are critical to all categories and that they can significantly affect the way customers perceive the organization.

The first category, reliability—which is concerned with service outcomes—consistently is rated the most important in meeting customer expectations. However, the other four categories (responsiveness, assurance, empathy, and tangibles) have been found to be most important in exceeding customer expectations. For more information on the five dimensions of service, refer to Handout 13–1 and to the discussion of customer expectations in chapter 11.

Distribute Handout 13–1: Categories of Customer Expectations. Pair people up to discuss their answers for 10 minutes. Bring the group back together, share the correct answers, and see if any issues or questions arise. Suggest that people continue to think about ways to meet customer expectations. You can recommend that they talk about the questionnaire in team meetings back at work and keep a running list of the customer expectations that they observe.

Handout 13–1

Categories of Customer Expectations

Len Berry and his team of researchers at Texas A&M University have determined that the following five categories are most critical in showing that you care about customers and in meeting customer needs.

1. **Reliability:** Capability to deliver the service that was promised in a dependable and accurate way.
2. **Responsiveness:** Eagerness to help customers and deliver prompt service.
3. **Assurance:** Skill, knowledge, and courtesy of employees, and their ability to solve problems confidently and convey trust.
4. **Empathy:** Caring, individual attention, and relationship building extended to customers.
5. **Tangibles:** Products, services, and the appearance of buildings, facilities, and equipment.

How do we show that we care? The questions below will encourage you to consider customer needs and what it takes to meet those needs.

Instructions: For each scenario below, write the evident customer need (reliability, responsiveness, assurance, empathy, tangibles) in column A. In column B, write "Yes" or "No," depending on whether you think the need was met. If the need was not met, write down what could have been done to meet the need.

SCENARIO	COLUMN A CUSTOMER NEED	COLUMN B WAS THE NEED MET? WHAT WOULD YOU HAVE DONE?
1. A computer company offers a special price in an advertised computer sale. When customers get there, they are told the company had only one in stock and it was sold.		
2. A customer asks a server which is better, the meatloaf or the turkey. He says, "I don't know. I just work here."		
3. A customer arrives at a store five minutes before closing to buy an item needed for the next day. The salesperson says, "You'll never make it; that item is in the back of the store and we close in five minutes."		

continued on next page

Handout 13–1, continued
Categories of Customer Expectations

SCENARIO	COLUMN A CUSTOMER NEED	COLUMN B WAS THE NEED MET? WHAT WOULD YOU HAVE DONE?
4. A customer enters a bank building that has breathtaking décor and tasteful signs directing her to the right area.		
5. A customer is buying a new digital camera but has no idea how digital cameras work. The salesperson says, "Don't worry. It takes some time to learn, but you'll do it. I know how frustrating new technology can be. Let me show you how to get started."		
6. An employee is having a bad day at work. Knowing that she sometimes gets a cup of coffee to revive, her boss offers to bring her some coffee.		

Answer Key:

1. Reliability
2. Assurance
3. Responsiveness
4. Tangibles
5. Empathy and assurance
6. Empathy

Learning Activity 13–4: Benefits

GOALS

The goals of this activity are

- ◆ to identify individual customer service strengths
- ◆ to brainstorm the benefits of delivering fantastic service
- ◆ to review individual benefits
- ◆ to review company benefits.

MATERIALS

The materials needed for this activity are

- ◆ PowerPoint slides: "Benefits!" (slide 11), "Satisfying the Customer" (slide 12)
- ◆ Handout 13–2: Benefits (optional).

TIME

- ◆ 5–15 minutes

INSTRUCTIONS

Option 1

Show the "Benefits!" slide. Discuss the benefits of delivering exceptional service. Do this as a brainstorming session. Participants should come up with personal as well as organizational benefits. Then show the "Satisfying the Customer" slide to summarize and to reinforce what the group has discussed.

Option 2

Show the "Benefits!" slide. Distribute Handout 13–2: Benefits and give participants five minutes to fill it out. Have them discuss their answers in pairs for five minutes. Bring the group together to summarize pair discussions. Show the "Satisfying the Customer" slide to summarize and to reinforce what the group has discussed.

Handout 13–2

Benefits

Instructions: Record your answers to the following questions in the spaces provided below.

1. What are your best customer service skills?

2. What benefits do you receive for providing superior service?

3. How does your superior work benefit the organization?

Learning Activity 13–5: Governing Forces

GOALS

The goals of this activity are

- to present forces that govern customer service

- to compare systematic forces that are not within the control of participants with those that are within their control.

MATERIALS

The materials needed for this activity are

- PowerPoint slide: "Customer Service: Governing Forces" (slide 13)

- Handout 13–3: Governing Forces in Customer Service

- flipchart and marking pen.

TIME

- 5–35 minutes

INSTRUCTIONS

Option 1 (5 minutes)

Show the "Customer Service: Governing Forces" slide. Briefly review the material on the slide. Refer to Handout 13–3 for your own reference. Highlight some issues for the class to address.

Option 2 (20–35 minutes)

Distribute Handout 13–3: Governing Forces in Customer Service. You may have individual participants do any one of the following:

- Read and answer the questions on the handout before you review the areas.

- Read the handout after you review the areas.

- Use the handout as a reference.

Discuss the governing forces. Ask for comments regarding each area. Use the questions on the handout as a guide and record comments on a flipchart. If participants fill out the handout, ask how they identified personal improvement areas. This can be a lively discussion, especially if participants have much to say about the organization and their levels of satisfaction with organizational procedures. The comments that you record on the flipchart can be used to indicate areas in which an organization might improve customer service.

Comments that come up in this discussion may include the following:

- ◆ There is no job training; we are expected to learn everything on the job.

- ◆ Expectations change.

- ◆ Management team members need to work on their interpersonal skills.

- ◆ People don't work together in the organization; departments are competitive.

- ◆ Procedures change all the time; nobody knows what they are.

- ◆ There is not enough emphasis on professional growth.

Ask participants their perception of the problems and what they would like to see changed in each category. If you will be taking their comments back to management, let the class know that. If this is not a part of the plan, ask them how they can help the organization move in a positive direction in the areas that you have discussed. Examples might include the following efforts:

- ◆ Mentor people who are new to the organization.

- ◆ Set up a buddy system for training.

- ◆ Ensure that your own attitude is always positive.

- ◆ Promote teamwork.

- ◆ Help others in the organization.

- ◆ Think of ways to improve procedures.

- ◆ Recommend changes that are well researched.

- ◆ Have discussions at team meetings to address what type of exceptions can be made to policy, and what is acceptable to the supervisor in charge.

- ◆ Take professional development courses that are offered at work or take them outside of work to ensure that you have updated skills.

   ◆ Be proactive.

   ◆ Present ideas that are good for the customer and good for the organization.

Variation

Form teams to answer the questions, record the answers on flipchart paper, and present them to the group.

KEY POINT

Although some procedures may not be as customer-friendly as participants would like, their own attitudes and behaviors can greatly influence customer satisfaction—even in situations that are less than optimum.

Handout 13-3
Governing Forces in Customer Service

Instructions: There are several key governing forces that affect customer service: mastery, positive attitude, healthy procedures, and shared vision and teamwork. Review the descriptions of those forces below and then answer the questions about how those forces are evident in your organization. Write down ideas about how you might improve in these areas.

Mastery: *Job Skills*

1. A desire to know and understand your job, why you do it, and how your role is important to others

2. Adequate training when you enter the company and ongoing training to update your job and technical skills

3. Knowledge and understanding of expectations

4. Desire to learn and practice new skills

5. Willingness to mentor others

6. Cross-training.

Mastery: *Communication Skills*

1. Continuously refining and practicing skills necessary to communicate effectively (including listening, empathizing, solving problems, flexibility, presenting a positive image, resolving conflicts, expressing appreciation, providing feedback, and offering support)

2. Practicing skills with internal customers and external customers.

Positive Attitude

1. Acting as an enthusiastic representative of your organization with commitment and genuine respect for others

2. Understanding that if you are positive, customers will be more positive

3. Acting with positive intent, courtesy, and goodwill

4. Being able to change your mindset to produce positive results

5. Knowing that attitude is all up to you—a good attitude is contagious!

Healthy Procedures

1. Having well-defined procedures to follow, with enough flexibility for you to work in the best interests of the organization and the customer

2. Knowing where to go for exceptions

3. Being able to get help with explanations

4. Understanding what decisions you can make and when you need approval

5. Using your empowerment to foster organizational goals and customer loyalty.

continued on next page

Handout 13–3, continued
Governing Forces in Customer Service

Shared Vision and Teamwork

1. Working as a team to realize the vision, mission, and goals of the organization
2. Constantly improving
3. Learning about other departments and how all areas of the organization work together for quality service
4. Embracing different personalities and opinions
5. Involving everyone in the decision-making process.

QUESTIONS ABOUT GOVERNING FORCES

Mastery: *Job Skills*

1. Is it important to you to do the best job you are capable of doing?

2. Do you have the job skills you need?

3. Are you clear about what is expected of you?

4. Does the organization have a job training program?

5. If not, how do you receive training?

6. How do you contribute to mentoring new employees?

7. Are there opportunities for professional growth?

8. Do you want to learn new skills for your own personal satisfaction and continued success?

9. What courses do you take to learn new ways to improve your performance?

10. What books and trade publications do you read?

11. Do you ever surf the net to find out ways to improve your organization or your performance?

continued on next page

Handout 13–3, continued

Governing Forces in Customer Service

Recommendations for improvement:

Mastery: *Communication Skills*

1. Are you given opportunities to develop your communication skills?

2. What kinds of training are offered?

3. Does a coach mentor you on your communication skills?

4. Do you think about areas in which you would like to improve?

5. Do you practice?

Recommendations for improvement:

Positive Attitude

1. Do you have a positive attitude?

2. Do you always try to show your positive attitude, even when you are having a bad day?

Recommendations for improvement:

Procedures

1. Are you aware of all the procedures you need to know to provide good customer service?

continued on next page

Handout 13–3, continued

Governing Forces in Customer Service

2. How are you informed about changes in procedure?

3. What procedures do you think limit your ability to provide good customer service?

4. Can those procedures be changed?

5. What would you have to do to change procedures that are not customer-friendly?

Recommendations for improvement:

Shared Vision and Teamwork

1. Do you have a clear idea of the direction in which your organization is going?

2. Do you know your company's vision, mission, and goals?

3. What does your organization do to keep you informed of new directions?

4. Do you have opportunities to contribute to the goal-setting process for your area?

5. What communication procedures does your organization use to ensure that everyone has an opportunity to contribute ideas?

6. How well do people work together?

7. How well do you work with people who are different from you?

Recommendations for improvement:

Learning Activity 13–6: Moments of Truth

GOALS

The goals of this activity are

- to provide an opportunity for participants to think about their own customer service experiences

- to identify negative customer service behaviors

- to determine if negative behaviors exist in their own organizations

- to discuss moments of truth.

MATERIALS

The materials needed for this activity are

- PowerPoint slides: "Moments of Truth" (slide 14), "Your Worst Customer Service Experience" (slide 15), "Caring Is the Greatest Gift" (slide 16), "Handling Moments of Truth" (slides 17–19)

- Handout 13–4: Worst Experience

- flipchart and marking pen.

TIME

- 20 minutes

INSTRUCTIONS

Explain that when customers seek out an organization, they have expectations, as discussed in Learning Activity 13–3: Customer Expectations. Those expectations are present at all times and at all levels. In each moment of contact with an organization, a customer is forming an impression. Moments of truth begin when customers are driving around looking for a parking place, and end when they leave the premises.

Moments of truth are not cumulative. Customers do not evaluate their entire experience with an organization. Although a customer has 98 good experiences, if the 99th is negative, the customer may say, "This is the last time I'm coming here," or, "I'm going to tell everyone I know about this place." Point out that moments of truth happen every second in an organization.

Show the "Moments of Truth" slide. Say, *"Here are some moments of truth that could be either positive or negative."*

Tell the class that sometimes it is helpful to think of their own customer service experiences to get an idea of how other people might feel when they receive poor service.

Show the "Your Worst Customer Service Experience" slide and give these directions: *"I would like you to think of your own customer service experiences and how you might have received poor service at one time or another. Think of a particularly bad experience that occurred outside of your work environment. You are going to pair up and share your experience with a partner."*

Before you distribute the handout and pair them up, instruct participants to think of

1. their worst customer service experience in recent months

2. what took place

3. how they were treated by the service provider

4. their response to poor service

5. the likelihood that they will return to the place where the incident occurred

6. how many people they told about the incident.

Distribute Handout 13–4: Worst Experience. Give participants a few minutes to think about an experience and record notes on the handout. If some participants cannot think of a situation, they may choose one of the two scenarios included in the handout and describe how they would feel in that situation. Allow three minutes for recording and reading.

Point out to participants that nobody wants to be treated in an inconsiderate manner. Customers don't want to wait in long lines only to be helped by someone who is rude. They don't want unmet promises and excuses. Nobody cares about company policies and rules when they want their service needs met. They want representatives to be responsive to their needs. The scenarios included in the handout help illustrate those simple truths.

Put participants in pairs. If you have an extra person, form a trio. Tell participants that they each have two minutes to describe the situation, and that their partners will be listeners. Instruct listeners just to listen—not evaluate or jump in and tell their stories before the first speakers are finished.

Begin the exercise. Circulate. Make sure that people are listening and not interrupting. Call time after two minutes and have partners switch roles. After five minutes, bring the group back together. Ask what actual behaviors made their experiences so negative or annoying. Examples might include

- being kept on hold too long

- rudeness

- being ignored

- an impatient or disinterested tone of voice.

Encourage participants to be as specific as possible while you record their responses on a flipchart. Summarize the exercise by saying that the behaviors they do not like are the same behaviors their own customers do not like.

Ask, *"Do you see evidence of these behaviors in this organization?"* Take a few answers to the question.

HANDLING MOMENTS OF TRUTH

Although moments of truth happen all of the time, it is important to address and try to reverse negative outcomes. Some ways to handle unsuccessful or negative moments of truth are

- to show that you care

- to apologize

- to go out of your way to fix the problem.

Show and discuss the "Caring Is the Greatest Gift" and the "Handling Moments of Truth" slides. Explain that you will be discussing ways to avoid moments of truth in subsequent training activities.

This is a good time to show one of the videos listed in the Resources section of this book. Keep in mind that showing a video will extend the time required for this activity.

Handout 13–4

Worst Experience

Instructions: Sometimes drawing from your own experience is the best way to learn. Think about your own recent customer service experiences and answer the questions below. If you have had no applicable experiences, read the two scenarios included here, select one, and answer the questions that accompany it.

1. Describe the worst customer service experience you have had in recent months.

2. What took place?

3. How did the service provider treat you? What was your response?

4. Will you return to that setting?

5. What do you think are common complaints about customer service?

CUSTOMER SERVICE SCENARIOS

Scenario 1: Dealership Blues

You take your car to the dealership where you bought it because the driver's side window is stuck (a problem that is under warranty). You expect to be greeted by someone who knows you because you have been very faithful about bringing the car in for service check-ups.

You go to the service desk. Several attendants are talking to each other behind the counter. Nobody says "hello" or acknowledges you. The service attendant directly in front of you does not look up. He is writing an order for the last customer in line. You ask if it will be long. He says, "I'll get to you when I get to you," still not looking up.

When he does finally look up, you tell him the problem. He says, "What did you do to make the window jam?" You say, "Nothing." He looks at you like you are a criminal lying to a jury. He writes up the order on your car without speaking to you at all. Then he says, "You can pick the car up day after tomorrow."

You say, "But I need the car tomorrow. I brought it in first thing this morning so you could work on it. I called and your technician told me that it could be done in one day."

"Well, he was wrong" he says. "Do you want us to fix it or not? I've got other people waiting."

continued on next page

Handout 13–4, *continued*
Worst Experience

"I have to meet a customer tomorrow morning 50 miles from here," you tell him. "I rearranged the customer appointment so I could meet him tomorrow instead of today because you promised I would have the car tomorrow."

He says, "Sometimes we're just plum out of luck, aren't we?"

Questions:

1. How would this scenario make you feel?

2. Would you return to that location for service?

3. Might such an incident influence whether you would purchase another car at that dealership?

Scenario 2: Policy Rules

You've had a tough morning, and you didn't have a chance to eat breakfast. At 11:15 you decide to take a break before the lunch crowd hits the local restaurants. You walk out of the office and see a fast-food place with only a few people in line. When you get to the counter, you say, "I'd like the breakfast special." The server says, "It's too late for breakfast. We stop serving breakfast at 11:30."

"But I was here at 11:30," you say, "and you have plenty of breakfast meals right behind you in the heated bin."

The server says, "It's our policy to stop serving breakfast at 11:30."

You say, "Well, what are you going to do with the breakfast meals behind you?"

"Throw them away," the server says. "Pick something from our lunch menu or leave. And hurry up. I have to take a break before the lunch crowd arrives."

Questions:

1. How would this scenario make you feel?

2. What would you do?

3. Would you return to this place in the future?

4. Are you likely to patronize another location of this fast-food restaurant?

Learning Activity 13–7: Fantastic Service Equation

GOALS

The goals of this activity are

- ◆ to introduce the Fantastic Service Equation
- ◆ to familiarize participants with equation components.

MATERIALS

The materials needed for this activity are

- ◆ PowerPoint slide: "Fantastic Service Equation" (slide 20)
- ◆ Handout 13–5: The Fantastic Service Equation.

TIME

- ◆ 10 minutes

INSTRUCTIONS

Show the "Fantastic Service Equation" slide. Explain the equation in this way: *"To provide a foundation for positive customer experiences, we will be using the Fantastic Service Equation to identify elements of communication that are necessary for fantastic service every time. We say 'every time' because it's important that service be outstanding every time, not just sometimes.*

"We will be looking at the different elements of this equation in detail. The framework gives you a way to think of what you probably already do naturally. It is a reminder of the steps or components that lead to excellent service in most circumstances.

"The Fantastic Service Equation will help in our quest to let customers know that we care, no matter how difficult the situation. It also will help ensure that we give that extra little bit that we otherwise might not think to do."

Distribute Handout 13–5: The Fantastic Service Equation and discuss it.

Handout 13–5

The Fantastic Service Equation

Equation Components

1. Greeting the customer
2. Determining needs
3. Meeting needs
4. Making the moment memorable
5. Checking results
6. Leaving the door open

Component 1. Greeting the Customer. Responsive service starts with a responsive greeting. You only get one first chance to impress a customer, and that first chance lasts only a matter of seconds. Customers expect a friendly greeting, complete with eye contact, a smile, and receptive body language. It's basic: A greeting recognizes a person's worth right off the bat and establishes rapport. A proper greeting immediately says, "I'm here to serve," which is what service is all about.

Greetings come in all forms. A parking lot attendant might say, "Glad to see you today!" A security guard might open the door for you in the morning, walk you to the elevator, and push the button for your floor. Greetings are given by the librarian who says "hello" and smiles before you do, and by the customer service representative who answers the phone with a smile and means it when she says, "How can I help you today?"

Component 2. Determining Needs. Finding out what a customer needs determines the rest of the interaction. Listening and asking questions are fundamental to this part of the equation. Listening can help with sales, with customer concerns, and with solving problems. Proactive listening is the key ingredient in providing responsive, empathic service. When you listen, give the customer your undivided attention and respect. Proactive listening involves total concentration, paraphrasing, and understanding thoughts and feelings—working together with the customer for everyone's benefit.

Component 3. Meeting Needs. When needs are determined, it's time to act. Responding effectively includes acting quickly and with confidence, and figuring out what you can do to make the customer happy. It requires giving the customer what was promised, finding out information, delivering a product or service on time, being available to answer a question or answer the phone, and guiding the customer toward a solution.

Component 4. Making the Moment Memorable. Here's where your creativity comes into play. This is where you do something special. It could be something big or something little. Whatever it is, it makes the customer feel good. Creating a memorable moment could be as simple as walking someone to her destination rather than pointing or telling her where

continued on next page

Handout 13–5, continued

The Fantastic Service Equation

to go. It could be staying after hours to complete a transaction. It could be calling a customer up to see if the solution you agreed on worked. It could be checking the installation of equipment you sold.

There are many great stories of memorable moments. We all have them. Some of them are grapevine stories that have become customer service folklore—legends passed on from generation to generation of customer service advocates. Consider this one: Nordstrom's, a department store that is well known for outstanding service, once had a disgruntled customer come in with a defective tire. The store gladly took the tire back and refunded the customer's money. What's so unusual about this story? Nordstrom's doesn't sell tires.

Component 5. Checking Results. There is an easy way to see if you are giving fantastic service. Just ask. Companies and organizations spend a lot of money on surveys, comment cards, and other means of soliciting customer feedback. But frontline workers can be the first to get feedback simply by asking, "How was our service today?" Even asking with sincerity, "Is there anything else we can do for you?" is a way to see if all the customer's needs have been met.

You can promote other services when you check results. You can offer the option of another service or you can tell a customer something he didn't know about your organization. Checking results helps solidify the relationship with the customer and improves your organization's image in the customer's eyes.

Responses may not always be positive. When you ask for their opinions, customers may complain. A complaint, however, is just an opportunity. It points you toward things to make better and ways to improve. Handling a complaint can be a memorable moment.

> **Key Point:** *A complaint is a memorable moment waiting to happen. Research shows that customers who complain and get their complaints resolved satisfactorily are actually more loyal than if they had no problem at all.*

By involving customers in your organization and asking about their opinions you pave the way for customer loyalty.

Component 6. Leaving the Door Open. There are many ways to encourage customers to return to your organization. Customers like to be appreciated. Leaving the door open is a way to say, "Please come back," or "Thanks for your support." It is a way to recognize them and support their patronage. You might say,

- ◆ "Thanks for being our guest here."
- ◆ "Hope you come back to buy your next birthday present."
- ◆ "Call me personally if you have any more questions."
- ◆ "I'll be looking forward to seeing you when you come back with the information we talked about."

Learning Activity 13–8: Greeting Group

GOALS

The goals of this activity are

- ◆ to emphasize the importance of greetings

- ◆ to demonstrate the power of a smile and eye contact.

MATERIALS

All that is needed for this activity is

- ◆ a room large enough for people to get up and move around.

TIME

- ◆ 5 minutes

INSTRUCTIONS

Use this exercise to demonstrate greeting, the first element of the Fantastic Service Equation.

Ask participants, *"How do you feel when you are not greeted? How do you feel when you walk up to a retail counter and two people are talking and they ignore you? How do you feel when someone says 'Next!' and doesn't look at you?*

"Greeting customers is one of the most important customer service behaviors to get right the first time. A face-to-face greeting should include a smile and eye contact. Even over the phone, a greeting should include a smile. Research shows that although you can't see the customer on the other end, you can actually hear a smile over the phone. Think about how you feel when someone smiles at you. It's hard not to smile back. Let's see this in action."

Give participants the following directions: *"I would like everyone to get up and greet every person in the class with a smile and eye contact. Please do this nonverbally. Everyone up!*

"Make sure you greet everyone with a smile and eye contact. Some people may want to shake hands. This is fine. If anyone isn't smiling, make a special effort to go to that person and smile."

When it looks as if nearly everyone has greeted everyone else, say, *"When you have greeted everyone, you may sit down."*

Discuss the exercise briefly. Give the group some feedback on what you saw. Usually you will see that everyone in the room smiled. Ask them how it feels to be greeted warmly.

Variation

If you do not have room for people to move around, they may greet each other with a smile and eye contact while sitting in their seats.

Learning Activity 13–9:
Determining Needs: Communication

GOALS

The goals of this activity are

- to emphasize the importance of listening in determining customer needs

- to practice paraphrasing

- to practice empathizing

- to practice questioning.

MATERIALS

The materials needed for this activity are

- PowerPoint slides: "Determining Customer Needs Requires Two-Way Communication" (slide 21), "Listening" (slides 22 and 23), "Demonstrate Proactive Listening" (slide 24)

- Handout 13–6: Listening

- Handout 13–7: Paraphrase the Thought, Validate the Heart

- flipchart and marking pen.

TIME

- 45 minutes

INSTRUCTIONS

This activity presents useful information about communication and proactive listening. It includes some brief lectures on key concepts. There also are exercises to reinforce the content you present. You may use these exercises together or as short, independent activities, depending on the timeframe within which you are working.

Communication

Communication is essential to all parts of the Fantastic Service Equation, so it is important to consider how communication works. To communicate, two people must perceive the same message. This requires the sender of the message to be clear in delivering the content and intent of the message, and the receiver to listen and understand the message. It requires two-way communication.

Show the "Determining Customer Needs Requires Two-Way Communication" slide.

Explain, *"Roy Lantz, trainer and consultant, compares communication to a fax machine. If you send a fax and the other person doesn't get it, have you communicated? Similarly, if you send an email and another person doesn't open it, or misunderstands it, have you communicated?*

"In face-to-face and telephone communications, the most important aspects of the communication process are listening and responding. Although listening is the most basic ingredient in the communication process, it can be the most difficult.

"Everyone involved in the communication process must understand each other fully, in words, intent, and meaning, including ideas and emotions."

Show the "Listening" slides. Ask, *"What cues do people give to indicate that they are really listening to you?"* Record responses on a flipchart.

The Two Levels of Listening

Explain, *"There are two levels of listening. One involves listening to thoughts; the other involves feelings, or 'listening to the heart.'"*

Listening to Thoughts

Explain, *"Listening to thoughts involves hearing what a person is telling you about a situation, such as a description of events or facts. Sharing thoughts is what goes on in most conversations. A good way to show customers that you are listening to their thoughts is to repeat what they have said, or to paraphrase it."*

Repeating what a customer has said may include introductory phrases such as the following:

- ◆ "Now let me see if I got this right . . . "

- ◆ "I just want to be sure I understand . . . "

Paraphrasing is similar to repeating; however, you put the customer's statement in your own words, or you use your own words to clarify parts of a statement. Ask participants when they think paraphrasing might be helpful. Paraphrasing helps make sure that you get the right message—what the customer really means. This does not require a lot of words, but it does require listening for the right message. To show participants what paraphrasing means, at some point during your explanation of paraphrasing, ask them to paraphrase what you just said.

To practice paraphrasing, run the following exercise as a whole-group activity, with pairs being observed by the entire group. Everyone can benefit from observing others. Here is what you do:

1. Have each person think of a common customer interaction.

2. Direct two people who are sitting next to each other to pair up for a role play.

3. Have person *A* do a quick role play of the interaction she chose, playing the customer.

4. Have person *B* paraphrase what the customer said.

5. Have person *A* determine if person *B* got the message.

6. Discuss the experience. Point out if person *B* jumps right to solving the problem without paraphrasing the situation. If the message was not received accurately, ask person *B* if he would like help to figure out how to paraphrase what person *A* said. Allow others to help.

7. Have the pair switch roles, with person *B* role playing the situation and person *A* paraphrasing. Debrief again.

Here is an example of such an interaction:

Customer: I came here at eight o'clock and nobody was at the desk. This happens a lot. I want to know who's the boss around here.

Customer service professional: Are you saying you came here at eight and nobody was here to help you?

Continue with pairs modeling different scenarios for about 10 minutes. Because paraphrasing is critical to listening, spend enough time on this exercise to have most people practice. You may assign some scenarios to two participants, or you can play the customer and have a participant paraphrase what you say.

Is paraphrasing important? We often jump into solving problems without having all the information we need. Paraphrasing is a learned skill that helps you get the information you need to move to the next step. Counselors use this technique to ensure that they understand their clients. Service providers need to learn the same skill to ensure that they are receiving the correct information, and that customers feel understood.

Participants may tell you that they have tried paraphrasing and that people have said that they sound like parrots, or customers have gotten annoyed and said, "I just told you that!" Explain that genuine interest and a sincere tone of voice are necessary for effective paraphrasing. Encourage them to use their best judgment to figure out when it is appropriate to paraphrase.

Listening to the Heart

Explain, *"To hear a message adequately, we need to listen to both the thought and the heart. Feelings often are not as easily communicated as thoughts. Nonetheless, recognizing a customer's feelings is a powerful communication tool. When you listen to the heart, you can validate a person's perspective, and learn about what he or she is feeling about what is being said."*

Next, ask for a list of feelings commonly expressed by customers. The group should identify some common feelings, such as happy, confident, sad, angry, or frustrated. How is it possible to know what customers might be feeling? Empathizing and asking questions can help identify customers' feelings and build trust. Empathizing with a customer means putting yourself in his or her shoes. Phrases that convey empathy include the following:

- ◆ "I can understand how you feel."

- ◆ "I'm sorry that happened."

- ◆ "You must be very angry."

Empathy differs from sympathy in that the focus is on the other person. If you say, "Yes, that happened to me once," and draw the attention back to yourself, you are sympathizing. Sympathizing is not very helpful in customer situations because customers don't want to hear about you. They want you to listen to them.

Asking Questions

There are times when we need additional information from customers, or we need to clarify the information that they have given us. In these cases, open-ended questions are most helpful. Open-ended questions require answers that provide you with facts, details, or other information. Open-ended questions include

- ◆ Can you tell me more about...?

- What else. . . ?

- What happened. . . ?

- How did. . . ?

- What would happen if. . . ?

Frequently we need simple answers. In those situations, it is best to ask closed-ended questions. Closed-ended questions solicit short, quick, "yes" or "no" answers. Closed-ended questions may begin with

- Are you. . . ?

- Do you. . . ?

- Can you. . . ?

- Would. . . ?

- Did. . . ?

Ask your participants, *"What are some examples of closed-ended questions?"* Here are some examples:

- Did you get the letter we sent?

- Did you pay your bill last month?

- Would you like me to make that call for you?

Explain, *"Whether you use open- or closed-ended questions depends on whether you want to control the information you are receiving, whether you want more information, and whether you have time for elaboration. Asking an open-ended question such as, "What happened?" can provide new information and influence how you view a situation. It also provides an opportunity for others to describe their perceptions of the situation or conflict.*

"Asking closed-ended questions enables you to control the conversation and reduce rambling, but it's a skill to use only when you have enough information to know what questions to ask."

Proactive Listening

Show the "Demonstrate Proactive Listening" slide. Summarize listening skills by saying that proactive listening involves paying attention to both thoughts and feelings, and it sets the stage for problem solving. The following are features of proactive listening:

- Giving your full attention

- Projecting sincerity verbally and nonverbally

- Paraphrasing

- Responding with empathy

- Asking open-ended and closed-ended questions.

Distribute Handout 13–6: Listening. Allow 20 minutes for the activity. If you have time for another exercise on this topic, distribute Handout 13–7: Paraphrase the Thought, Validate the Heart. This is an optional exercise for practicing paraphrasing and questioning.

Handout 13–6

Listening

Instructions: Think of a situation that you have had with a customer, or a common work scenario that you have had some difficulty handling. It should be a problem that has the potential for resolution. Describe the situation and your feelings about it in the spaces provided, and then follow the directions below with a partner.

1. What is or was the scenario?

2. What feelings do you or did you have about it?

Discussion Directions:

- ◆ Take five minutes to discuss your scenario and your feelings with your partner. Remember that you will not be trying to solve the problem.

- ◆ Your partner will listen, paraphrase, empathize, and ask questions only. If he or she begins to tell you what to do, or asks leading questions (for example, "Don't you think you should...."), make a "T" (time-out) sign with your two forefingers. Continue when your partner goes back to just listening.

- ◆ After five minutes, let your partner evaluate how well he or she implemented the proactive listening guidelines.

- ◆ Give your partner feedback on how you think he or she listened.

- ◆ Switch roles and begin again.

Handout 13–7

Paraphrase the Thought, Validate the Heart

Instructions: Below are four customer comments. Read each and, in the spaces provided, write down the responses you would make to the customers' perspectives. Remember to ask yourself

- ◆ what is the customer feeling?
- ◆ what is the real message the customer is conveying?
- ◆ how will you paraphrase the thought, validate the heart, and ask questions? (For example, would you ask open- or closed-ended questions?)

Here's an example:

Customer: I have called your organization eight times in the last two hours. Each time I got voice mail and pressed "O" for operator like the instructions said, I got someone else's voice mail. When I pressed "O" again, I got disconnected!

Response: You must be very frustrated. I'm so sorry you weren't able to get through.

1. "My health is important to me. I need to get approval to see another doctor and I'm hoping that this won't take too long. I just found out that I need a referral and I want to make this appointment next week when I have a day off from work."

   Response:

2. "You billed me on my credit card and I didn't get the merchandise I ordered. I'm hoping that this mistake can be corrected and that I can get my order. I've never had this problem with your company before."

   Response:

3. "I bought this dress here two weeks ago and I want to return it. It just doesn't fit. I don't know if I gained weight or if the dress shrunk. I paid a lot of money for this dress and I want my money back!"

   Response:

4. "I'm not sure I'm in the right place. I'm not sure I got the right directions."

   Response:

Learning Activity 13–10: Noise

GOALS

The goals of this activity are

♦ to present the concept of "noise"

♦ to have participants consider how their own thoughts and feelings may get in the way of communication.

MATERIALS

The materials needed for this activity are

♦ PowerPoint slides: "What Gets in the Way" (slide 25), "Noise" (slides 26 and 27), "Curtain Down" (slide 28)

♦ Assessment 12–2: Noise Detector.

TIME

♦ 15–25 minutes, depending on whether you use the assessment

INSTRUCTIONS

Explain that you are going to take a look at why people don't always listen well. Sometimes "noise," including mental and environmental factors, hinders our ability to listen.

Show the "What Gets in the Way" and "Noise" slides. Discuss the factors described below. Emphasize the scripts we run in our minds when confronted by various distractions.

Environmental Distractions

In any work environment there are telephones ringing, people talking in the background, and continuous interruptions. Regular noise can make it difficult even to hear clearly, so listening becomes an even greater challenge.

Filters

All of us filter our perceptions of other people. Filters are like screens, and they can affect our ability to be receptive and to listen. They also sometimes involve stereotypes, whether we consciously recognize them or not. Stereotypes and assumptions can be triggered by dress, language, accents, religion, and other differences. Filters also may make us more receptive to people who are like us.

Values

Our values define who we are. Values are what we cherish and act on—they include integrity, honesty, devotion to family, and achievement. Conflicts in values can arise among customers and co-workers, and they can make it difficult to listen to the other person.

Other Noise Factors

- ◆ **Contact overload:** Too many contacts in a day can cause exhaustion.

- ◆ **Mind clutter:** Thoughts about voice messages, emails, and things to do at home can be distracting.

- ◆ **Lack of interest:** When one hears many complaints of the same kind, it can be difficult to stay interested.

- ◆ **Tone of voice:** High-pitched, low-pitched, angry, impatient—a tone of voice can be disconcerting, especially when the speaker appears critical.

- ◆ **Misinterpretation:** When a misunderstanding has occurred, it is more difficult to listen because each party wants to get his or her point across.

- ◆ **Evaluation/jumping to conclusions:** Judging what someone is saying instead of listening carefully can take an interaction off track.

Distribute Assessment 12–2: Noise Detector. After participants have filled out the assessment, put them into pairs or trios to discuss what they would like to improve. Tell them to be sure to listen and paraphrase. Give each person five minutes to talk while the others listen proactively. Call time after five minutes and have them switch roles. Be sure to circulate to manage the interactions. If participants need more time, extend the time.

Show the "Curtain Down" slide. Explain, *"It is important to figure out what types of noise you experience in the communication process, work to listen without any distractions, and close the curtain on the noise."*

Another option: Have participants write on a piece of paper any noise they have in their minds and then fold the paper. Tell them that you would be glad to help them stop the noise by having them put their papers in a safe place (a box) if they would like to get rid of it. They can pick the noise up at the end of class if they still want it!

Learning Activity 13–11: Body Language

GOALS

The goals of this activity are

- ◆ to demonstrate the importance of body language in communicating with customers

- ◆ to practice behaviors that are easily communicated without words.

MATERIALS

The materials needed for this activity are

- ◆ PowerPoint slides: "What Else Gets in the Way?" (slide 29), "Body Language" (slide 30)

- ◆ index cards (for optional activity).

TIME

- ◆ 10 minutes

INSTRUCTIONS

This activity can be done in a variety of ways. You can use the suggestions in this exercise or you can include games similar to charades to convey the fact that body language is an important part of communication.

Explain, *"Another way to communicate to customers about whether we are paying attention to their concerns involves body language. Body language is very powerful. Communications experts say that over 90 percent of our messages have little to do with the actual words we use. That means that how we deliver a message is as important as what we say. How do we deliver messages to customers? How do customers let us know their feelings through their body language? Think of body language behaviors that give you a clue to how a customer feels."*

Show the "Body Language" slide. Ask what messages the behaviors described on the slide might deliver. Discuss.

Variations

- ◆ For a game similar to charades, write emotions on index cards (one emotion on each card). Ask for several volunteers to act out the emotions and distribute cards to them. Have them act out the emotions in front of the class and have the class guess the emotion.

◆ Ask the class what types of body cues irritate them the most. Have them act out the body language they describe.

◆ Put people in pairs and have them tell each other what his or her body language has been saying throughout the training session.

Learning Activity 13–12: Positive Language

GOALS

The goals of this activity are

- to change the paradigm from "what you can't do" to "what you can do"

- to practice changing negative statements into positive statements.

MATERIALS

The materials needed for this activity are

- PowerPoint slides: "No I Can't/Yes You Can" (slide 31), "Why Are These Negative?" (slide 32), "How to Hit a Foul" (slides 33 and 34), "Positive Language: What Can You Do?" (slide 35), "How to Say 'No' When You Must" (slide 36)

- Handout 13–8: Positive Language

- flipchart and marking pen.

TIME

- 20–25 minutes

INSTRUCTIONS

Explain the "can-do" attitude described in Handout 13–8: Positive Language. Can-do statements help ward off negative customer perceptions and pave the way for fantastic service scenarios. Worst-case scenarios often can be avoided with just the power of positive language.

Show the "No I Can't—Yes You Can" slide. Explain that a tug-of-war inevitably happens when someone says, "No I can't," because a customer's immediate response is, "Yes you can." Depict such a conflict in one of these ways:

- Play a tug-of-war game here. Have a rope available and split participants into two teams for a quick tug.

- Stage an arm-wrestling match.

◆ Have people try to get a piece of candy from one another. Tell the partner with the candy, "You can't give the candy up," and instruct the other to plead verbally, using any reason he or she can think of to convince the partner to give up the candy.

Show the "Why Are These Negative?" slide. Tell participants that it is better to explain a policy or procedure and its benefits than merely to say, "It's company policy." If you don't know the reasons behind company policies, find out about them so you can offer appropriate explanations to customers.

Show the first "How to Hit a Foul" slide. Ask participants for other responses they find offensive. Write responses on a flipchart. Show the second "How to Hit a Foul" slide, and emphasize that negative messages can be communicated through body language, as well as verbal language.

Show the "Positive Language" slide. Ask for other examples. Show the "How To Say 'No' When You Must" slide. Discuss it with participants.

Distribute Handout 13–8: Positive Language. Note that an answer key is provided for you to reference in case you need to provide suggestions. You may use the handout in a couple of ways.

Option 1

◆ Form pairs. Have participants work together to develop positive statements.

◆ Allow five to 10 minutes for pairs to complete the handout.

Option 2

◆ If you have limited time for this exercise, form teams and assign a different statement on the handout to each team.

◆ Have the teams share their positive statements with the rest of the group.

Handout 13–8

Positive Language

Turning a bad situation into a good one can be as easy as telling a customer what you *can* do instead of what you *can't* do, or as simple as apologizing for an unavoidable inconvenience. The art of using positive language requires concentrating on how you communicate. In positive communication, you don't blame people—you solve problems.

Instructions: Turn the following questionable statements into better ones by using more positive language. Write your improved version in the space to the right of each statement. Here is an example:

Questionable: You didn't fill out the paperwork properly.

   Better: Let me help you with that part so we can process this right away.

QUESTIONABLE STATEMENT	MORE POSITIVE STATEMENT
Serving External Customers	
1. Our lines have been busy. We can't talk to everyone at once. What's your account number?	
2. That's wrong information. Who told you that?	
3. Didn't you read the sign? This is the wrong department for that concern.	
4. No, we don't do that sort of thing here. We're not Community Services.	
5. You should have come earlier. We close at 4:30.	
6. You have to know your serial number before we can fix your equipment.	
7. You should have known that we needed written permission before we could send that document.	
8. That's the policy. If you call before 3:00, we can process your request the same day. It's 3:05.	

continued on next page

Handout 13–8, continued

Positive Language

QUESTIONABLE STATEMENT	MORE POSITIVE STATEMENT
Serving Internal Customers 9. I don't have time to answer your questions now. 10. You don't need to know that. Just do your job. 11. Why are you always late with the information I need? It holds me up with customers. 12. I can't help you. It's not my department. Maybe accounting or finance can help. Their numbers are in the book. 13. You're new here? Lots of luck. We all had to learn the hard way. 14. You are always late. We have to pick up your slack and answer your department's questions when we don't even know the answers.	

Answer Sheet on next page

Handout 13–8, continued

Positive Language

Answer Sheet

Here are some examples showing how to transform negative language into positive language and improve the questionable statements above.

QUESTIONABLE STATEMENT	MORE POSITIVE STATEMENT
Serving External Customers	
1. Our lines have been busy. We can't talk to everyone at once. What's your account number?	I'm so sorry you had to wait. Thank you for your patience. Let me try to get what you want as quickly as possible so you don't have to wait any longer. If you give me your account number, I can see your history and help you more quickly.
2. That's wrong information. Who told you that?	Let me make sure you have the correct information. I need to clarify a point.
3. Didn't you read the sign? This is the wrong department for that concern.	Let me show you where you can get that information.
4. No, we don't do that sort of thing here. We're not Community Services.	We have a division called Community Services that would be glad to help you with that. Let me call them and tell them you're coming.
5. You should have come earlier. We close at 4:30.	Allow me to help you so that you can get what you need before we close, or if necessary, we'll be happy to help you first thing tomorrow.
6. You have to know your serial number before we can fix your equipment.	We can fix your equipment. If you give me your serial number, it will make it easier for me to determine how to do it.
7. You should have known that we needed written permission before we could send that document.	I can get you the person who can authorize that for you.
8. That's the policy. If you call before 3:00, we can process your request the same day. It's 3:05.	This will be processed first thing tomorrow.

continued on next page

Handout 13–8, continued
Positive Language

QUESTIONABLE STATEMENT	MORE POSITIVE STATEMENT
Serving Internal Customers	
9. I don't have time to answer your questions now.	What can I help you with? May I get back to you in five minutes so I can give you my full attention?
10. You don't need to know that. Just do your job.	It's useful to know a variety of skills and to be able to focus on your responsibilities as well.
11. Why are you always late with the information I need? It holds me up with customers.	It would help the customers (and me) if I could get the information I need on time.
12. I can't help you. It's not my department. Maybe accounting or finance can help. Their numbers are in the book.	Let me call accounting for you and see if they can help. If not, let's call finance.
13. You're new here? Lots of luck. We all had to learn the hard way.	I know how it is to be new. Let me show you how to do that.
14. You are always late. We have to pick up your slack and answer your department's questions when we don't even know the answers.	Being on time will help us a lot. You have the right information and we need you to make sure that customers are getting the correct information.

Learning Activity 13–13: Dealing with Anger

GOALS

The goals of this activity are

- ◆ to discuss how to deal with angry customers

- ◆ to present the "Stages of Frustration."

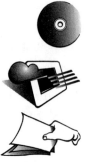

MATERIALS

The materials needed for this activity are

- ◆ PowerPoint slides: "Stages of Frustration" (slide 37), "Dealing with Anger" (slide 38), "Positive Language" (slide 39)

- ◆ Handout 13–9: Dealing with Anger

- ◆ flipchart and marking pen.

TIME

- ◆ 10 minutes

INSTRUCTIONS

Explain, *"Sometimes circumstances will cause a customer to become upset or angry, even when you have done your best to meet his or her expectations. When dealing with emotions, it is easy to fall into the trap of becoming emotional yourself."*

Distribute and review Handout 13–9: Dealing with Anger. Show the "Stages of Frustration" slide. Explain the stages as they are described on the handout.

Participants often want to know what they should do when customers are outright abusive. Show the "Dealing with Anger" slide and discuss it. On a flipchart, draw a line that represents a continuum with the words "courteous" and "abusive" on either end and "okay" in the middle. Ask the group what percentage of customers fall into each category on the continuum. This illustration is to help participants recognize that most customers are not abusive, although people have a tendency to remember difficult customers.

Nonetheless, a very angry customer can be a real problem. The bottom line is that nobody is expected to take abuse. Here are some suggestions for dealing with inappropriate behavior:

◆ Follow company guidelines on physical abuse and violence in the workplace.

◆ Tell the customer that you would like to help, but you would appreciate receiving the same level of respect that you are giving to him or her.

◆ If swearing, abusive cursing, or insulting continues, feel free to say, "I think it would be better for someone else to help you," and call a supervisor or colleague.

◆ Never hang up on a customer. However, if real abuse is occurring over the phone and the techniques above do not work, it is acceptable to say, "I think we will need to talk about this at another time. Would you like me to call you back?" or "I'm going to have to hang up, but feel free to call me back when you think we can work this out together." Check company policy regarding telephone etiquette for further guidance.

Show the "Positive Language" slide. Use the examples on the slide to demonstrate how to be assertive without being aggressive.

Variations

Option 1:

◆ Distribute Handout 13–9: Dealing with Anger. Tell participants that they will be doing role plays later, and that in their role plays they will be asked to demonstrate the guidelines for dealing with anger that are discussed in the handout.

Option 2:

◆ Use the handout in conjunction with Learning Activity 14–5: The Angry Customer.

◆ Distribute Handout 13–9: Dealing with Anger. Form teams of five. Have the teams write on a flipchart those behaviors that they find most difficult to handle, and how they handle the difficult behaviors. Have teams present their examples to the larger group.

Handout 13–9
Dealing with Anger

When dealing with emotions, it often is easy to become emotional yourself. To avoid this trap, remember the following points:

1. Angry people may be used to receiving hostile responses when they exhibit hostile behavior. Responding in an angry manner, however, will create a win-lose situation (where someone wins and someone else loses). You want to achieve a win-win solution.

2. Don't take the anger personally. Look at the angry response as a communication and a problem that needs to be resolved.

3. Remember that feelings are never right or wrong. They are just feelings.

4. Be confident, not aggressive. Use statements that let the customer know that you are confident and assertive. Aggression will only make matters worse; confident behavior will help set the tone for mutual problem solving.

5. Recognize that people who are angry go through stages of frustration. Stage one is feeling helpless or powerless. Stage two is feeling restrained or frustrated. Stage three is the full anger stage. It is difficult for people in the third stage to listen because actual physiological responses, including an increase in adrenaline, are taking place.

6. Make sure you follow listening guidelines because listening is the most important skill in dealing with anger. Often, if someone who is upset sees that you care enough to listen to his or her problem, the anger dissipates and the person is able to move toward a solution. Be sure to offer empathy and support and to validate ideas and feelings.

7. Practice "sorting," a listening technique that isolates the problem at hand by ignoring sarcasm, exaggeration, and personal attacks.

Learning Activity 13–14:
Meeting Needs: Problem Solving

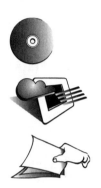

GOALS

The goals of this activity are

- ◆ to describe the steps of problem solving

- ◆ to give participants an opportunity to practice problem solving.

MATERIALS

The materials needed for this activity are

- ◆ PowerPoint slides: "Meeting Needs" (slide 40), "Problem Solving" (slides 41–43)

- ◆ Handout 13–10: Problem Solving

- ◆ flipchart and marking pen.

TIME

- ◆ 25 minutes

INSTRUCTIONS

Show the "Meeting Needs" and "Problem Solving" slides. Discuss the steps of problem solving. Emphasize the importance of follow-up and the fact that the number-one expectation of customers is that you will do what you say you are going to do.

Option 1

Distribute Handout 13–10. Have people pair up. Refer participants to the problem they worked on when they completed Handout 13–6: Listening during Learning Activity 13–9. Instruct them to work with a partner to resolve the issue they described in that handout.

Option 2

Ask one of the participants to share the problem he or she described on Handout 13–6 during Learning Activity 13–9. Have the whole group help the participant resolve the issue, using the problem-solving guidelines described in Handout 13–10. Use a flipchart to work through the problem.

Handout 13–10

Problem Solving

Instructions: Consider a customer problem you have dealt with in the past (you might want to refer to the problem you described on Handout 13–6: Listening). Follow the problem-solving guidelines below to find new ways to address the issue. In the space following each of the guidelines, describe how you would correct the difficulty.

1. **Define the problem.** Separate it from its emotional content.

2. **State the problem as clearly as possible.** If there is more than one issue, define each issue separately.

3. **Describe what you can do and what your limitations are.** Use positive language and informative explanations to describe
    - what you will do to satisfy the customer
    - when you will do it
    - how you will do it
    - why you will do it
    - who will be involved
    - where it needs to be done
    - what your limitations are.

4. **Agree on a solution.** Provide alternatives, if appropriate.

5. **Verify the solution.** Ask if the solution is acceptable and summarize agreements.

6. **Follow up.** Follow up on what was promised. *The number-one expectation of customers is that you will do what you say you are going to do.*

Learning Activity 13–15: The Final Equation Components

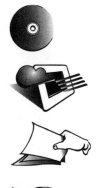

GOALS

The goal of this activity is

- to recognize how to make the moment memorable, check results, and leave the door open.

MATERIALS

The materials needed for this activity are

- PowerPoint slide: "The Final Equation Components" (slide 44)

- Handout 13–11: Final Equation Components.

TIME

- 10 minutes

INSTRUCTIONS

Tell a memorable-moment story of your own or use the examples below. Remind participants that making the moment memorable does not have to be something extraordinary. It just has to *feel* extraordinary to the customer.

MEMORABLE-MOMENT EXAMPLES: ADDING A SPECIAL TOUCH

Ann and Tony

Ann and Tony own a dry cleaning establishment. They know most of their customers by name, as do the rest of the staff. When people come in, no matter how busy they are, they greet the customers and usually remember to ask something specific, such as, "How's your mom doing?" If a button falls off a garment or a hem is loose, they repair it at no charge. They always put out a bowl of candy for people to enjoy, and they help customers carry cleaning to their cars.

Great Teas

When a new tea company began selling their products in Dede's hometown, she had a hard time finding the brand. She wrote to the company and they sent her a list of places where she could buy the teas in her area. They also sent her a case of 24 extra-large cans of tea in assorted flavors. Her response was, "Now that's good customer service, and well beyond what was expected!"

A Touch of Warmth

When the shoes Margery ordered from a mail-order company arrived, there was a small ivory-colored envelope in the box. The printed message on the front of the enclosed card read "Thank You for Your Business" and there was a neat handprinted message inside.

> *Dear Margery,*
>
> *We would like to thank you for shopping with us online. We really appreciate your business, and hope you like the shoes that you ordered. We look forward to serving you again in the future. Thank you.*
>
> *Sincerely,*
>
> *Carl's Footwear*

Margery's response was, "The impact of that note on me was incredible. The coldness of the Internet was suddenly warmed up with this very sweet note. Why would I ever shop elsewhere?"

Just Checking

Mimi's car wouldn't start. She happened to be close to a gas station, so she walked there to find assistance. One of the station attendants walked back to the car with her and tried to jump-start it. It didn't work. He tried troubleshooting, using everything he knew, but no luck—the car still would not start. Mimi thanked him and called AAA. On his way home, the attendant stopped by just to see if she was okay. She was so appreciative, she wrote his boss a letter of thanks.

Distribute Handout 13–11: Final Equation Components. Instruct participants to complete the form in relation to a scenario they already have discussed.

Handout 13–11
Final Equation Components

Instructions: Using a customer service scenario you already have discussed, describe how you could realize each of the last three components of the Fantastic Service Equation (making the moment memorable, checking results, and leaving the door open). Also describe the possible organizational benefits of realizing these components of the equation.

FANTASTIC SERVICE COMPONENT	ACTION EXAMPLES	ORGANIZATIONAL BENEFITS
Make the moment memorable		
Check results		
Leave the door open		

Learning Activity 13–16:
Putting It All Together: Role Playing

GOALS

The goals of this activity are

- ◆ to give participants an opportunity to practice positive customer service skills

- ◆ to provide feedback to participants on how they use the skills in a role-play situation.

MATERIALS

The materials needed for this activity are

- ◆ PowerPoint slide: "Role Plays: Putting It All Together" (slide 45)

- ◆ Handout 13–12: Role Plays

- ◆ Handout 13–13: Fantastic Service Equation Observation Form.

TIME

- ◆ 60–80 minutes

INSTRUCTIONS

The instructions for this activity assume that there has been some discussion of the behaviors that are necessary for excellent customer service, such as those that are described in the Fantastic Service Equation.

Explain, *"Now it's time to put it all together. Using the Fantastic Service Equation, you will be role playing some scenarios that are common in your organization. Put all that you've learned to work for you, and see how really outstanding you can be in providing fantastic service to customers."*

Distribute Handout 13–12: Role Plays. Put the class into groups of five or six and give the following instructions:

"You each have a scenario that you have worked on. In your group, come to consensus to pick one scenario that you would like to role play. It should be one in which a customer is angry, confused, or annoyed. You will be role playing in front of the rest of the class." (If participants have not worked on their own scenarios, each group can devise a situation to role play.)

"You have 15 to 20 minutes to develop your scenarios and to choose someone in your group who will be the service provider and someone who will be the customer. You may have more than one customer and more than one service provider if the situation calls for it. Everyone must participate in developing the scenario and in suggesting how to handle the situation based on the Fantastic Service Equation." (It is not necessary for everyone on the team actually to role play in front of the class. Some will only help in developing the scenario.)

"Make sure that your interactions in your scenario reflect the positive behaviors that we have discussed here today. Start your discussion now, and I will be available to help if you need me."

Circulate around the room to make sure everyone understands the directions. Each group will be role playing only one scenario, so suggest that they make a selection quickly. After you have circulated and helped them start, move two chairs into the middle of the room to set the stage for the role plays.

At 10 minutes, remind the groups that they have five minutes left (or 10, if they seem to need it), and that they should make sure that all the elements of the equation are covered.

Call time when the groups are ready. If there is a group that hasn't completed the assignment, you may have to call time anyway and have them ad lib the scenario.

Distribute Handout 13–13: Fantastic Service Equation Observation Form. Instruct participants to evaluate the teams based on the Fantastic Service criteria. Ask them to take notes on what is being said or done for each category.

Have the first team come to the stage. Ask the member who is playing the service provider to describe the situation briefly. Then have the team begin the role play.

As the role play unfolds, listen for negative phrases such as "no," "we can't," and the other phrases that you discussed in "How to Hit a Foul" (in Learning Activity 13–12: Positive Language). If you hear negative phrases, stop the role play and ask for a replay, or wait until the end of the scenario and then discuss better responses.

After each role play, ask all of the participants how well the service provider followed the equation. Ask them to give specific examples of where they saw the Fantastic Service Equation at work.

Continue until all role plays have been completed. If you have more time, do more role plays, giving the teams just a short time to prepare.

Handout 13–12

Role Plays

Instructions: Pick a scenario that identifies a common situation that occurs at work. You will be role playing the scenario in front of the class, using all elements of the Fantastic Service Equation. One member of your team should play the role of a customer who is angry, confused, or annoyed, and another should play the role of a customer service provider. If your scenario calls for it, others may play team member or supervisor roles.

In the spaces provided below, describe how you would accomplish each component of the Fantastic Service Equation in this scenario. Practice with your team before you perform your role play in front of the class. The class will be evaluating your performance, so review the criteria on the observation sheet (Handout 13–13) to ensure that you cover all aspects of the equation.

Scenario:

◆ Greeting:

◆ Determining needs:

◆ Meeting needs:

◆ Making the moment memorable:

◆ Checking results:

◆ Leaving the door open:

Handout 13–13
Fantastic Service Equation Observation Form

Instructions: On a scale from 1 to 5, evaluate role-playing teams in relation to the criteria listed below. Circle the appropriate number.

1. Greeting Customer

   ◆ Smiled

   ◆ Had good eye contact

   ◆ Had receptive body language

   Comments:

   Not So Good   **Excellent**
   1   2   3   4   5

2. Determining Needs

   ◆ Repeated or paraphrased thoughts and feelings

   ◆ Empathized

   ◆ Asked appropriate questions

   Comments:

   Not So Good   **Excellent**
   1   2   3   4   5

3. Meeting Needs

   ◆ Was helped by problem-solving guidelines

   Comments:

   Not So Good   **Excellent**
   1   2   3   4   5

4. Making the Moment Memorable

   ◆ Added a special touch

   Comments:

   Not So Good   **Excellent**
   1   2   3   4   5

continued on next page

Handout 13–13, continued

Fantastic Service Equation Observation Form

5. Checking Results

   ◆ Asked for feedback

   Comments:

Not So Good				Excellent
1	2	3	4	5

6. Leaving the Door Open

   ◆ Promoted products or services

   ◆ Asked customer to return

   ◆ Thanked customer

   Comments:

Not So Good				Excellent
1	2	3	4	5

Learning Activity 13–17: Customer Service Action Plans

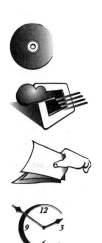

GOALS

The goals of this activity are

- to have participants determine a course of action to take in continuing their practice of excellent customer service

- to commit to action.

MATERIALS

The materials needed for this activity are

- PowerPoint slide: "Thanks for Attending" (slide 46)

- Handout 13–14: Customer Service Action Plans.

TIME

- 15 minutes

INSTRUCTIONS

Briefly review what you have gone over in the workshop. Explain that in this exercise participants will determine how they will use the principles you've discussed when they are back on the job. Give the following instructions:

"Please take 10 minutes to write down how you plan to enhance your skills back at work so you can deliver fantastic service every time."

Distribute Handout 13–14: Customer Service Action Plans. Explain the action plan components and instruct participants to complete the handout. After 10 minutes, call the class back together. Ask for a few volunteers to share what they will do back at work. Then ask if there were any other insights that people learned from the workshop.

Show the "Thanks for Attending" slide. Thank participants for their efforts in the program and recognize them for their interest in achieving fantastic customer service every time.

Handout 13–14
Customer Service Action Plans

Instructions: In the spaces below, follow the directions to describe what you will do to improve your ability to deliver excellent service.

1. I will take the following actions to provide fantastic customer service.
   List the actions that you will carry out to improve the customer service climate of your organization.

2. To accomplish my customer service goals, I will seek out the specific help and support I need.

   Identify the type of assistance you will need, if any. Will you need the cooperation of other staff, of your boss?

3. I plan to accomplish these goals by a specific date.

   Set a date for completion. If the activities will be ongoing, write "ongoing," and decide when you will begin the process.

4. I will evaluate my progress.

   Evaluation is essential to recognizing whether or not objectives have been met. Describe the method(s) you will use (for example, customer satisfaction surveys, performance evaluations, and other plans for measuring progress).

Optional Learning Activities

♦ Nine learning activities

♦ Five handouts and other materials

This chapter includes learning activities that are not included in the designs for one-hour, half-day, and one-day training sessions presented in chapters 7, 8, and 9. These activities can be substituted for those presented in chapter 13 or they can be used as stand-alone exercises. Like other activities in this workbook, they can be modified to fit specific training needs and the amount of time available.

Learning Activity 14–1:
Bad News: Unacceptable Service

GOALS

The goals of this activity are

- to raise awareness about the effects of productive and counterproductive behaviors in feedback situations

- to generate commitment to an action plan for improving unacceptable feedback.

MATERIALS

The materials needed for this activity are

- Handout 14–1: Bad News Scenario

- Handout 14–2: Effective and Ineffective Feedback

- Handout 14–3: The Jones Window.

TIME

- 30 minutes for exercise

- 30–60 minutes for the debriefing

INSTRUCTIONS

This exercise can be used with supervisors or modified for frontline staff. Form groups of five to seven participants. Seat the groups away from each other to minimize distractions. Distribute Handout 14–1: Bad News Scenario and instruct participants to study it silently.

When all participants have read the scenario, distribute Handout 14–2: Effective and Ineffective Feedback. Assign at least one quadrant in the matrix to each group. Instruct the groups to discuss the scenario above and fill in their assigned quadrants of the matrix. Encourage them to carry out this task by seeking consensus before recording entries.

Thanks to John E. Jones, distinguished author and consultant, for permission to include this exercise in the workbook.

When all groups have completed their parts of the matrix, reassemble them into a large group for reporting. Have a member of each group report to the large group while others take notes in the proper quadrants. At this point participants should ask questions for clarification but withhold reactions.

Facilitate a general discussion of each quadrant. In addition to asking for reactions and comments, raise the following questions:

1. What does poor feedback cost in terms of employee morale, loyalty, and the quality of customer service?

2. How can we keep from engaging in ineffective behaviors in critical feedback situations?

Distribute Handout 13–3: The Jones Window and instruct participants to work silently while making action plans for themselves. Call for volunteers to share their plans with the whole group.

Note: The Jones Window is a valuable tool that can be used with customized scenarios in any part of this training program. You can write your own scenarios and use the window to review appropriate and inappropriate ways to respond to common workplace situations and sensitive workplace issues.

Variations

♦   Edit the scenario to fit local situations more closely. Do not use actual occurrences or real people in your scenario.

♦   Use more than one scenario—perhaps one per group.

♦   Use a buddy system to construct the action plan. Have participants select a partner and assist each other in completing the plan, or have buddies present the plans of their partners rather than their own.

♦   Establish a rule of "what is said here stays here," and facilitate a discussion of real feedback situations and the real people involved. Actual names need not be used.

KEY POINTS

You may choose to make the following points if they do not emerge spontaneously during the group discussion:

♦   Feedback should state the observed event clearly and should not involve personal attack.

- ◆ Feedback should almost never take place in the presence of other people.

- ◆ Two-way communication is the first skill to suffer in the feedback situation. Good listening techniques tend to go away first.

- ◆ Feedback should never take place when a supervisor is angry.

- ◆ Feedback should be brief and to the point. Do not say, "Yes, and another thing. . . ."

Handout 14–1
Bad News Scenario

Consider the following example of unacceptable feedback:

> Several customer service specialists work in the same office, within earshot of each other. They wear telephone headsets but they can hear whatever happens in the room. All report to the same supervisor, who can listen in on their telephone interactions with customers and consult with any of them by telephone or in an adjacent office.

> One of the customer service specialists gets involved in a rather heated exchange with a customer. The specialist refuses to investigate the customer's concerns and finally says to the customer, "You know, you're a real pain to do business with!"

> Because everyone can hear half of this conversation, they all stop and listen. The supervisor overhears the conversation as well and marches straight to the customer service specialist's desk. "What the hell are you up to?" the supervisor asks. "You just cost us a customer! I won't put up with your negative attitude anymore. Either you call that customer back and apologize, or you're outta here."

Questions:

1. How did the customer service specialist step over the line?

2. How might the specialist have better handled the situation with the customer?

3. To what degree did the specialist deserve negative feedback regarding the exchange with the customer?

4. How would you react to the supervisor's behavior in this situation?

5. How might the supervisor have handled this situation differently?

6. How might the customer service specialist protect his or her rights in this situation?

Handout 14–2

Effective and Ineffective Feedback

Instructions: Use this worksheet to record your group's recommendations in the selected quadrants. Make notes in the remaining quadrants during the reports from the other groups.

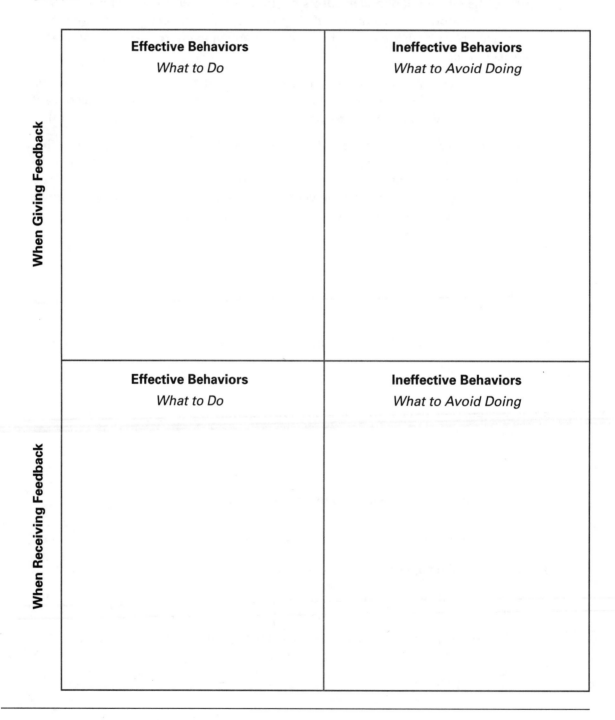

	Effective Behaviors *What to Do*	**Ineffective Behaviors** *What to Avoid Doing*
When Giving Feedback		
When Receiving Feedback		

Handout 14–3
The Jones Window—An Action Plan for Improvement

Instructions: Use this form to record your commitment to specific improvements in your ability to operate effectively in a feedback situation, either as a customer service specialist or supervisor. Be prepared to share your plan with the group.

As a result of what I became aware of in this session, I intend to . . .

Start Doing		Stop Doing
	Continue Doing	
Do More		**Do Less**

Learning Activity 14–2: Yes, and . . .

GOALS

The goals of this activity are

- ◆ to encourage participants to provide memorable moments for their customers

- ◆ to think "out of the box" about how to exceed customer expectations.

TIME

- ◆ 25 minutes

INSTRUCTIONS

"Yes, and . . . " is an improvisational technique that exaggerates positive responses to the point of the absurd. By focusing on what you *can* do, instead of what you can't do, the game encourages creative thinking and a can-do attitude.

Ask participants to think of ways they provide service through

- ◆ reliability

- ◆ responsiveness

- ◆ assurance

- ◆ empathy

- ◆ tangibles.

Form groups of three participants each. Instruct one participant in each trio to be the customer in a role play. The other two participants will compete to provide the best service to the customer. The role play will start with the customer saying, "I would like. . . ," "Could you get me . . . ," or some similar request.

Service provider *A* will answer "Yes, and. . . ," and will say another thing she or he can get to please the customer.

Service provider *B* then will build on *A*'s response and say, "Yes, and I can get you [repeat *A*'s last response] *and* [another item]." The back-and-forth exchange continues until the customer makes another request and the round begins again.

Demonstrate this exercise with someone in the class before you allow participants to practice in their trios. Here is an example:

Customer: "I would like a BLT."

Service provider A: "Yes, and I can get you a BLT and cole slaw with that."

Service provider B: "Yes, and I can get you cole slaw and a Coke."

Service provider A: "Yes, and I can get you a Coke and a straw."

Service provider B: "Yes, and I can get you a straw and a complimentary order of french fries."

Give participants ten minutes to practice in their trios. Ask trios to do their "Yes, and . . . " role plays in front of the class.

Variation

Have each person restate *all* of the items, not just the last one. For example, "I can get you a BLT, cole slaw, a coke, a straw, a complimentary order of french fries . . . and. . . ."

DEBRIEFING

Discuss how customers often want something special when they interact with service providers. Refer to the "making the moment memorable" component of the Fantastic Service Equation (Learning Activity 13–15: The Final Equation Components) if you previously covered that material.

Learning Activity 14–3: Moments of Truth II

GOALS

The goals of this activity are

- ◆ to demonstrate how moments of truth can be handled poorly

- ◆ to give participants a creative way to act out moments of truth.

MATERIALS

All that is needed for this activity are

- ◆ a flipchart and marking pen.

TIME

- ◆ 20 minutes

INSTRUCTIONS

Ask for two volunteers. Take the first volunteer out of the classroom and give her or him these directions: *"You are to demonstrate disinterest regarding whatever your partner is saying in the following exercise. Use your creativity to exaggerate boredom, fidget, and display a lack of consideration in any way you can."*

Take the first volunteer back to the classroom and ask the second volunteer to step out of the classroom with you. Give him or her these directions: *"Think of something that you are looking forward to doing. Explain to your partner what it is and how enthused you are about it."*

Go back into the classroom and ask both volunteers to come to the front of the class. Have them sit in chairs facing each other. Ask the second volunteer to describe something he or she is looking forward to doing. The first volunteer will follow your instructions, displaying complete disinterest.

Now ask the volunteer who tried to explain what he or she was happily anticipating to define the expectations he or she had when the exchange began and to give reactions to the behavior of the disinterested listener. Note the responses on a flipchart. Explain that expectations can lead to moments of truth. Discuss how responding to a customer can make or break a moment of truth.

To summarize the exercise for the class, review communication and the proactive listening guidelines outlined in Learning Activity 13–6: Moments of Truth and Learning Activity 13–9: Determining Needs.

Variation

Demonstrate the first scenario with the volunteers. After the demonstration, divide the group into pairs to complete the exercise. Have partners switch roles after three minutes.

When participants complete the exchange, debrief the activity asking the question, "What are you looking forward to?" Have one person speak first and the other paraphrase, ask questions, and empathize. Then have them switch roles. Bring the full group back together. Ask the pairs to describe the differences in the two perspectives.

Ask the group to describe circumstances in which it is especially important to paraphrase with customers. Write responses on a flipchart, and add the following circumstances to the list if they are not mentioned by participants:

- when giving directions
- when a person is upset
- when someone is rambling
- to confirm an order
- to validate feelings.

Learning Activity 14–4:
Role Playing Negative Responses

GOALS

The goals of this activity are

- ◆ to identify negative behaviors that produce negative results for customers

- ◆ to provide an opportunity to process interactions.

MATERIALS

The materials needed for this activity are

- ◆ PowerPoint slides: "How to Hit a Foul" (slides 33 and 34).

TIME

- ◆ 45 minutes

INSTRUCTIONS

Show the "How to Hit a Foul" slides. Divide the class into teams of five. Ask teams to create a negative customer scenario using negative phrases and body language, as described on the slides. Suggest that they use real examples or scenarios that are likely to occur in their organization.

Have one person in each group take the role of customer and one take the role of service provider. Others may also take customer and supervisor roles. There must be at least two players, but there may be as many as five.

Allow 15 minutes for groups to create their role play. Tell them that all members of the team must participate in creating the role play.

Circulate to make sure that teams are creating scenarios that they can role play in front of the class. After 15 minutes, ask if everyone is ready. If they need more time, give them five more minutes. Help any team that seems to be struggling. Then have each group present their role play for the larger group.

After each scenario, ask the person who played the role of customer the following questions:

1. What went wrong?

2. How did you feel?

3. What did you want to do?

4. Would you want to do business again with this organization?

Ask the whole group the following questions:

1. What did you see?

2. How did the customer respond?

3. Were the service providers helpful?

4. What should they have done?

Variations

◆ This exercise can follow Learning Activity 13–6: Moments of Truth or it can be used to augment other exercises or discussions.

◆ Turn negative scenarios into positive ones. To do so, have the same team members recreate the role play to demonstrate how they would conduct the scenario using the Fantastic Service Equation.

Learning Activity 14–5: The Angry Customer

GOALS

The goals of this activity are

- ◆ to identify some behaviors that angry customers demonstrate

- ◆ to role play ways to work with an angry customer.

MATERIALS

The materials needed for this activity are

- ◆ Handout 13–9: Dealing with Anger

- ◆ Handout 14–4: The Angry Customer.

TIME

- ◆ 20 minutes

INSTRUCTIONS

Distribute Handout 13–9: Dealing with Anger. Review the concepts presented there.

Distribute Handout 14–4: The Angry Customer. Form pairs. Have one person play *Carol* and the other person play *Mrs. Bree.* Then have participants switch roles. When everyone has completed the scene, have two people come to the front of the class to perform the role play for the whole group.

Ask the class to process the interactions. In addition to discussing the helpful behaviors described on the handout, participants also may mention the importance of tone of voice and sincerity.

Handout 14–4
The Angry Customer

Carol: "Hello, what can I do for you today?"

Mrs. Bree: "Probably nothing. I never get the help I need here." *(sarcasm)*

Carol: "I'm disappointed that we haven't been able to help you. Maybe I can do better today." *(empathy, paraphrasing)*

Mrs. Bree: "If you don't turn my water back on, I'm going to sue you." *(attack)*

Carol: "When was your water turned off, Mrs. Bree?" *(questioning, sorting out attack)*

Mrs. Bree: "Today. Do you think I'd let it stay off a week and then come in here?" *(sarcasm)*

Carol: "So it was turned off today. That must have been very disturbing. Please let me see what I can do." *(repeating, empathy, offering assistance, moving toward a solution)*

Mrs. Bree: "Just get the water back on."

Carol: "Are you up-to-date paying your water bill?" *(sorting out demand, questioning, getting more information to help solve problem)*

Mrs. Bree: "Listen, I told you all I have is aggravation with you people." *(exaggeration)*

Carol: "Again, it bothers me to hear that." *(empathy, sorting out exaggeration)*

Mrs. Bree: "I was out of town and just came back today. I have never been late on a bill. So, this time I was late. One time. Big deal. National crime." *(sarcasm, exaggeration)*

Carol: "Do you have your payment with you?"

Mrs. Bree: "Yes. Here."

Carol: "Thanks for bringing this in so quickly after you got back. We'll have your water on just as soon as possible. I'm really sorry for this problem. You're a very good customer." *(appreciation, empathy, solution, apology, expression of support)*

Mrs. Bree: "Okay."

Carol: "Thank you for your patience in helping us find a solution this time. Now, are there other areas that I can help you with? I want you to have a better feeling for us and I want to provide you with the best service we can." *(appreciation of customer, verification of solution, checking results)*

Mrs. Bree: "No, that's okay. Thank you for your help. Actually, the other problems I had occurred some time ago." *(admits exaggeration)*

Carol: "Well, if there is anything else I can do for you, I surely want to help. Thanks for coming in and I hope everything will be smooth sailing from here." *(leaving the door open, appreciation of customer, showing care)*

Mrs. Bree: "Thanks. 'Bye."

Learning Activity 14–6: Customer Types

GOALS

The goals of this activity are

- ◆ to raise awareness of different personality types

- ◆ to have participants identify their customer service preferences

- ◆ to explore how customers with different personality types have different needs.

MATERIALS

The materials needed for this activity are

- ◆ Myers-Briggs Type Indicator instrument (This activity is designed primarily for instructors who are certified to administer the MBTI questionnaire, but it also can be used without the instrument.)

- ◆ Handout 14–5: Different Customer Personalities

- ◆ Handout 14–6: Responding to Customer Types

- ◆ two flipcharts and marking pens.

TIME

- ◆ 1–2 hours

INSTRUCTIONS

Instructors who are familiar with the Myers-Briggs Type Indicator instrument may purchase it and distribute it to participants. (The MBTI questionnaire is a rich tool to use in training. For more information on this instrument see www.mbti.com.)

If you are not using the MBTI, distribute Handout 14–5: Different Customer Personalities. (Because the handout is not a validated instrument, it is meant to serve only as a guide to working with different personality types.) Using the handout, review the basic characteristics of each personality type with the group. Have each participant circle the customer behaviors on the handout that best describe him or her.

When participants have completed the MBTI questionnaire or Handout 14–5, they will have self-identified as one or the other of four personality-type pairs: extrovert/introvert, sensor/intuitive, thinker/feeler, and judger/perceiver. Divide the class four times into two groups. For example, begin by dividing participants into the self-identified extroverts and the self-identified introverts. Give the two groups the instructions below. After a period of discussion, bring the two groups back together and divide the whole class according to the next pair of dimensions. Repeat the process until all four pairs have been discussed in separate groups and the outcomes discussed by the whole group.

Directions for Groups

1. **Introverts/Extroverts:** Ask the two groups how they would like to be treated as customers, in relation to this category of preference. Have them list their desired modes of communication on a flipchart and then share this information with the other half of the class.

2. **Sensors/Intuitives:** Ask the two groups how they communicate as customers and how they would like to be treated as customers. Have them present their preferences to the larger group.

3. **Thinkers/Feelers:** Instruct each group to discuss and write down how they think *the other group* prefers to communicate and how members of that group would like to be treated (that is, have the thinkers come up with a list of how the they believe the feelers like to be treated as customers, and vice versa). Then have them present their findings to the opposite group and ask for feedback.

4. **Judgers/Perceivers:** Divide the class in two (or brainstorm with the whole class) to describe how judgers and perceivers might differ as customers.

Distribute Handout 14–6: Responding to Customer Types and discuss its contents with your training participants. The handout lists appropriate customer service behaviors responsive to the various customer personality types encountered on the job.

Handout 14–5
Different Customer Personalities

Instructions: Listed in the quadrants of the following chart are behaviors that might be exhibited by different customer types. Which behaviors do you exhibit when you are a customer? Put a checkmark in the box beside each behavior that might apply to you.

<table>
<tr><th colspan="2">Quadrant One</th></tr>
<tr>
<td>

EXTROVERT (E)—POSSIBLE BEHAVIORS

☐ Think out loud; talk thoughts out

☐ May repeat thoughts

☐ Get off topic

☐ Talk about personal experiences

☐ May tell the listener more than the listener wants to know

☐ Like to be sociable

☐ Are expressive

☐ May talk quickly

☐ Want feedback

Number of items checked: _____
</td>
<td>

INTROVERT (I)—POSSIBLE BEHAVIORS

☐ May tell part of the story and check to see if the service provider is listening

☐ May quietly wait to ask if the service provider can help

☐ Want to think through what you need to say before you communicate

☐ Want to develop rapport

☐ May respond slowly because you are thinking

☐ May not like to rock the boat

☐ May not want to bother the listener

Number of items checked: _____
</td>
</tr>
<tr><th colspan="2">Quadrant Two</th></tr>
<tr>
<td>

SENSOR (S)—POSSIBLE BEHAVIORS

☐ Want facts and figures

☐ Need to see things in black and white

☐ Take direction well

☐ Are good at detail

☐ May not see the whole picture

☐ Need solid evidence

☐ Want to know that the service provider has a well-thought-out plan

☐ Are suspicious of change

Number of items checked: _____
</td>
<td>

INTUITIVE (N)—POSSIBLE BEHAVIORS

☐ Like to see the big picture

☐ Are good at imagining possibilities

☐ Are creative

☐ Are interested in the future

☐ Do not like routine or lots of details

☐ Like to change things for the better

☐ Can jump in anywhere; don't go in order

Number of items checked: _____
</td>
</tr>
</table>

Scoring: When you have completed both parts of each quadrant, add up the checkmarks in both categories of each quadrant. The higher of the two scores in each quadrant determines which of the two personality characteristics in that quadrant best describes you. If the two scores in any quadrant are the same, decide which of the two sets of possible behaviors most accurately defines your likely behavior as a customer.

continued on next page

Handout 14–5, continued
Different Customer Personalities

THINKER (T)—POSSIBLE BEHAVIORS	**FEELER (F)—POSSIBLE BEHAVIORS**
☐ Are logical and usually think that you are right	☐ Want to establish rapport
☐ May tell the provider what to do	☐ Want to create solutions that are mutually agreeable
☐ May be impatient	☐ Have definite values
☐ Want immediate attention	☐ Are concerned about how decisions affect people
☐ Don't want to wait	☐ Want harmony instead of discord
☐ May give the impression that you don't think the service provider is capable	☐ May get feelings hurt or get angry if the service provider is abrupt
☐ Expect the service provider to fix problems	☐ Get upset with disrespectful treatment
☐ Want brief and concise answers	*Number of items checked:* _____
☐ May assume that the service provider should know what you want	
☐ Can act annoyed	
Number of items checked: _____	

Quadrant Three

JUDGER (J)—POSSIBLE BEHAVIORS	**PERCEIVER (P)—POSSIBLE BEHAVIORS**
☐ Need to know timelines	☐ Go with the flow
☐ Want to know when decisions will be made	☐ Are flexible
☐ Follow up on verbal deadlines	☐ May need to be reminded of deadlines and priorities
☐ Keep things in neat order	☐ Like to start things more than finish them
☐ Are not comfortable when things are left hanging	☐ Have piles of things all around; don't put a lot of value on being neat
☐ Need to have a well-thought-out plan	☐ Are spontaneous
☐ Don't like surprises	*Number of items checked:* _____
☐ Need to be prepared for changes	
Number of items checked: _____	

Quadrant Four

Write the characteristic on which you scored higher in each quadrant. Use the letters that appear in parentheses after each characteristic (for example, INFP): _____ .

Look at all of the behaviors you chose in all of the quadrants. Do they describe you as a customer?

Handout 14–6

Responding to Customer Types

Here are lists of customer service behaviors that are appropriate responses to the various customer personality types you may encounter in your job. Use these behaviors in providing excellent customer service.

How to Respond to Extroverts

- Listen.
- Paraphrase.
- Ask open-ended questions to build rapport and closed-ended questions to focus the discussion.
- Be congenial.
- Don't expect to come to conclusions right away.
- Suggest alternatives.

How to Respond to Introverts

- Greet with enthusiasm.
- Ask open-ended questions.
- Encourage communication.
- Allow time for responses.
- Don't interrupt.
- Be comfortable with silence.
- Spend time developing rapport.
- Reassure.

How to Respond to Sensors

- Give facts and details.
- Be practical and realistic.
- Show how things are similar to what they already know.
- Be clear and direct.
- Explain step-by-step what you are going to do.

How to Respond to Intuitives

- Give the overall picture first.
- Allow time for discussion.
- Validate their vision.

- Ask for their cooperation in filling out required paperwork.
- Repeat details you need to get across.
- Don't get frustrated.
- Walk them through it.

How to Respond to Thinkers

- Follow the listening guidelines.
- Use "I" statements (for example, "I can help you").
- Get things done quickly and accurately.
- Try to reach a decision cooperatively.
- Keep the person informed about what you can do.
- Offer alternatives, if appropriate.
- Be businesslike.
- Show you care.
- Be confident that you can help.
- Show that you are capable by your skillful actions.
- Create a win-win situation.

How to Respond to Feelers

- Be sincere and empathic.
- Show interest in what they are saying.
- Listen to concerns.
- Paraphrase.
- Be personable and friendly.
- Show that you care about their concerns.

continued on next page

Handout 14–6, continued

Responding to Customer Types

- Make sure your body language is receptive.
- Appreciate their suggestions.
- Validate their feelings.
- Involve them in decisions.

How to Respond to Judgers

- Have things in order.
- Make sure your deadlines are accurate.
- Follow up on commitments.

- Have a plan and follow it.
- Be clear about expectations.

How to Respond to Perceivers

- Try to be flexible.
- Don't get upset with lack of order.
- Help prioritize.
- Be clear about important deadlines.
- Allow flexibility when you can.
- Help in planning.
- Follow up with reminders.

Learning Activity 14–7: I'm Proud of . . .

GOALS

The goals of this activity are

- ◆ to identify individual strengths

- ◆ to appreciate partners.

TIME

- ◆ 10 minutes

INSTRUCTIONS

Tell participants that you would like them to think about what they are proud of in their roles as customer service providers. Ask them to pair with a partner. Allow 2.5 minutes for each person to describe his or her sources of pride to the partner. Bring the group back together and ask for volunteers to share their responses.

Variation

This learning activity can be used for an introductory or closing exercise. For introductions, you might open a session by asking, "What are you proud of and what do you want to improve?"

Learning Activity 14–8: Survivor

GOALS

The goals of this activity are

- to reinforce paraphrasing skills

- to determine how listening might be influenced by a vested interest.

MATERIALS

All you need for this activity is a set of

- index cards.

TIME

- 30–60 minutes

INSTRUCTIONS

Read the story below aloud to the group.

Survivor

Five people set out on a boat trip to Dream Island. Before they reach the island, the boat hits a large rock and breaks into pieces. They are able to swim to a deserted island. Eventually, a man in a small craft approaches and says he can take only one person with him and that there is no other way to safety. Only one of the people stranded will survive.

Ask five volunteers to come to the front of the room and sit in a line of chairs facing the group. Write each of the following roles on an index card and give a card to each of the volunteers. Tell volunteers not to share information about the characters they are portraying until it is their turn to speak. The roles are those of a

- scientist working on a cure for cancer

- pregnant mother receiving welfare assistance

- Pulitzer-Prize-winning journalist

- futurist working on trends that could influence the world's future quite positively

- felon just released from jail on a drug charge.

Tell the rest of the class participants that they will have to choose among the five characters seated in front the one who will be able to get on the boat and reach safety. Ask each of the five characters to role play making his or her case for being chosen to board the small craft. The characters can make up whatever they would like to describe their situation. After each person speaks, the next person must paraphrase what the last person has said. The audience then decides if the volunteer has paraphrased the last person well enough to tell his or her own story next. After all five characters have spoken, ask them to leave the room.

Give the participants in the classroom at least three minutes to select one person who will be rescued. Have them choose a representative to present their choice. Encourage them to commend all the role players for their presentations.

Bring the volunteers back in. Before the group's decision is announced, ask the role players the following questions:

1. How difficult was it to listen to the previous person and paraphrase when you had a vested interest in the outcome?

2. What "noise" did you experience? (Review Learning Activity 13–10: Noise.)

3. What did you talk about when you were out of the room? Did any feelings emerge?

4. When one of the volunteers paraphrased your statements, did it prompt you to think about more things to tell or to want to expand your story?

Ask the rest of the participants the following questions:

1. What initial reaction did you have to the different characters? Did their status in life influence your decision? Did any other noise make it difficult to listen?

2. Was the paraphrasing effective? Why or why not?

Have the class's representative explain whom they decided would be rescued and why.

Learning Activity 14–9: Superhero Exercise

GOAL

The goal of this activity is

- ◆ to give positive feedback to peers and internal customers.

MATERIALS

The materials needed for this activity are

- ◆ marking pens
- ◆ masking tape
- ◆ one sheet of flipchart paper per person.

INSTRUCTIONS

Usually this is done at the end of a training program to celebrate the team's accomplishments and to honor individual contributions. Explain that this is the "Superhero" exercise and its purpose is to give everyone positive feedback. If you have a large number of participants, form two teams and have two Superhero exercises going on at the same time.

Fold one sheet of flipchart paper in half for each participant. The paper will serve as a cape. Ask participants to line up and tape a cape to each person's back. Give everyone a marking pen. Have them circulate and write positive statements on others' capes (for example, "great participation," "terrific feedback," "wonderful role player"). Try to get everyone to write on each of the capes.

When everyone is finished, have them remove their capes at the same time and enjoy reading the feedback they've received.

Special thanks to Nancy Rehbine for allowing us to include this exercise.

Using the Compact Disc

Insert the CD and locate the file *How to Use This CD.txt.*

Contents of the CD

The compact di : that accompanies this workbook on training new supervisors contains three types of files. All of the files can be used on a variety of computer platforms.

- **Adobe .pdf documents.** These include assessments, handouts, and training tools.

- **Microsoft PowerPoint presentations.** These presentations add interest and depth to several training activities included in the workbook.

- **Microsoft PowerPoint files of overhead transparency masters.** This file makes it easy to print viewgraphs in black-and-white rather than using an office copier. They contain text only; no images to print in greyscale.

Computer Requirements

To read or print the .pdf files on the CD, you must have Adobe Acrobat Reader software installed on your system. The program can be downloaded free of cost from the Adobe Website, *www.adobe.com.*

To use or adapt the contents of the PowerPoint presentation files on the CD, you must have Microsoft PowerPoint software installed on your system. If you simply want to view the PowerPoint documents, you must have an appropriate viewer installed on your system. Microsoft provides various viewers free for downloading from its Website, *www.microsoft.com.*

Printing from the CD

TEXT FILES

You can print the assessments and handouts using Adobe Acrobat Reader. Simply open the .pdf file and print as many copies as you need. The following documents can be directly printed from the CD:

- Assessment 12–1: Customer Expectations
- Assessment 12–2: Noise Detector
- Assessment 12–3: Fantastic Service Every Time Survey
- Assessment 12–4: Secret Shopper
- Handout 10–1: Leadership and Customer Service
- Handout 10–2: Motivating Team Members
- Handout 13–1: Categories of Customer Expectations
- Handout 13–2: Benefits
- Handout 13–3: Governing Forces in Customer Service
- Handout 13–4: Worst Experience
- Handout 13–5: The Fantastic Service Equation
- Handout 13–6: Listening
- Handout 13–7: Paraphrase the Thought, Validate the Heart
- Handout 13–8: Positive Language
- Handout 13–9: Dealing with Anger
- Handout 13–10: Problem Solving
- Handout 13–11: Final Equation Components
- Handout 13–12: Role Plays
- Handout 13–13: Fantastic Service Equation Observation Form

- Handout 13–14: Customer Service Action Plans

- Handout 14–1: Bad News Scenario

- Handout 14–2: Effective and Ineffective Feedback

- Handout 14–3: The Jones Window—An Action Plan for Improvement

- Handout 14–4: The Angry Customer

- Handout 14–5: Different Customer Personalities

- Handout 14–6: Responding to Customer Types.

POWERPOINT SLIDES

You can print the presentation slides directly from this CD using Microsoft PowerPoint. Simply open the .ppt files and print as many copies as you need. You can also make handouts of the presentations by printing 2, 4, or 6 "slides" per page. These slides will be in color, with design elements embedded. PowerPoint also permits you to print these in grayscale or black-and-white, although printing from the overhead masters file will yield better black-and-white representations. Many trainers who use personal computers to project their presentations bring along viewgraphs, just in case there are glitches in the system.

Adapting the PowerPoint Slides

You can modify or otherwise customize the slides by opening and editing them in the appropriate application. However, you must retain the denotation of the original source of the material—it is illegal to pass it off as your own work. You may indicate that a document was adapted from this workbook, written and copyrighted by Maxine Kamin. The files will open as "Read Only," so before you adapt them you will need to save them onto your hard drive under a different filename.

Showing the PowerPoint Presentations

The following PowerPoint presentations are included on this CD:

- **One-Hour.ppt**

- **Half-Day.ppt**

- **One-Day.ppt**

Table A–1

Navigating Through a PowerPoint Presentation

KEY	POWERPOINT "SHOW" ACTION
Space bar *or* Enter *or* Mouse click	Advance through custom animations embedded in the presentation
Backspace	Back up to the last projected element of the presentation
Escape	Abort the presentation
B *or* b	Blank the screen to black
B *or* b *(repeat)*	Resume the presentation
W *or* w	Blank the screen to white
W *or* w *(repeat)*	Resume the presentation

Having the presentations in .ppt format means that they automatically show full-screen when you double-click on their filenames. You also can open them in Microsoft PowerPoint and show them from there.

Use the space bar, the enter key, or mouse clicks to advance through a show. Press the backspace key to back up. Use the escape key to abort a presentation. If you want to blank the screen to black while the group discusses a point, press the B key. Pressing it again restores the show. If you want to blank the screen to a white background, do the same with the W key. Table A–1 summarizes these instructions.

We strongly recommend that trainers practice making presentations before using them in training situations. You should be confident that you can cogently expand on the points featured in the presentations and discuss the methods for working through them. If you want to engage your training participants fully (rather than worrying about how to show the next slide), become familiar with this simple technology *before* you need to use it. A good practice is to insert notes into the *Speaker's Notes* feature of the PowerPoint program, print them out, and have them in front of you when you present the slides.

Resources

PRINTED MATERIALS

Albrecht, Karl. *Service Within*. Homewood, IL: Business One Irwin, 1990.

Anderson, Kristin, and Ron Zemke. *Delivering Knock Your Socks Off Service*. New York: AMACOM, 1998.

Beich, Elaine. *The ASTD Trainer's Sourcebook: Creativity and Innovation*. New York: McGraw-Hill, 1996.

Berry, Leonard L. *Discovering the Soul of Service*. New York: The Free Press, 1999.

—————, A. Parasuraman, and Valerie Zeithaml. "Improving Service Quality in America: Lessons Learned." *Academy of Management Executives,* volume 8, number 2, 1994.

—————. "Understanding Customer Expectations of Service." *Sloan Management Review Reprint Series,* volume 32, number 3, Spring 1991.

—————. "The Nature and Determinants of Customer Expectations of Service." *Journal of the Academy of Marketing Science,* volume 21, number 1, 1993.

Brinkerhoff, Robert O., and Anne M. Apking. *High Impact Learning: Strategies for Leveraging Performance and Business Results from Training Investments*. Cambridge, MA: Perseus Books, 2001.

Forum Corporation. "Customer Focus Research." *Executive Briefing*. Boston: Forum Corporation, 1988.

Gagne, Robert M., Leslie J. Briggs, and Walter W. Wager. *Principles of Instructional Design*. Fort Worth, TX: Harcourt, Brace, and Jovanovich, 1992.

Goodman, John. "Basic Facts on Customer Complaint Behavior and the Impact of Service on the Bottom Line." *Competitive Advantage,* June 1999.

Gross, T. Scott. *Positively Outrageous Service*. New York: Warner Books, 1991.

Jones, John E. "Don't Smile About Smile Sheets." *Training and Development Journal,* December 1990. Available for free at the Website http://ous.iex.net/SMILSHTS.HTM

Kaplan, Robert S., and David P. Norton. *The Balanced Scorecard*. Boston: Harvard Business School Press, 1996.

Kimbrough, Ralph B., and Michael Y. Nunnery. *Educational Administration: An Introduction*. New York: Macmillan, 1983.

Kirkpatrick, Donald L. "Developing Training Programs: Evidence vs. Proof." *Training and Development Journal*, November 1977.

Marrow, Alfred F. *The Practical Theorist: The Life and Work of Kurt Lewin*. New York: Basic Books, 1969.

Maslow, Abraham H. *Motivation and Personality* (3d edition). New York: Harper and Row, 1987.

McCarthy, Berenice. *About Learning*. Barrington, IL: Exel, 1996.

McGregor, Douglas M. *The Human Side of Enterprise*. New York: McGraw-Hill, 1960.

Naisbitt, John. *Megatrends: Ten New Directions Transforming Our Lives*. New York: Warner Books, 1982.

Naughton, Keith. "Tired of Smile-Free Service?" *Newsweek*, March 6, 2000.

Nelson, Bob. *1001 Ways to Reward Employees*. New York: Workman Publishing, 1994.

Phillips, Jack J. *Handbook of Training Evaluation and Measurement Methods*. Houston: Gulf Publishing, 1983.

Robbins, Stephen P. *Organizational Behavior* (9th edition). Upper Saddle River, NJ: Prentice Hall, 2001.

Roberts-Phelps, Graham. *Customer Relationship Management*. London: Hawksmere, 2001.

Senge, Peter M., Art Kleiner, Charlotte Roberts, Richard B. Ross, and Bryan Smigh. *The Fifth Discipline Fieldbook*. New York: Doubleday, 1994.

TARP (Technical Assistance Research Programs). *Consumer Complaint Handling in America: An Update Study, Part I*. Washington, DC: U.S. Office of Consumer Affairs, 1985.

—————. *Consumer Complaint Handling in America: An Update Study, Part II*. Washington, DC: U.S. Office of Consumer Affairs, 1986.

—————. *Consumer Complaint Handling in America: An Update Study, Part III*. Washington, DC: U.S. Office of Consumer Affairs, 1986.

Zemke, Ron, and Thomas Kramlinger. *Figuring Things Out: A Trainer's Guide to Needs and Task Analysis*. Reading, PA: Addison-Wesley Publishing, 1987.

FILMS

These excellent films can be used to augment or reinforce the programs included in this workbook. All films listed below are available from CRM Learning. Call Sue Caughman at 800.421.0833, extension 143, and mention code number 05MK01 to receive free previews, discounts, and a complimentary copy of *Harvard Business Review*'s "What Makes a Leader?" by Daniel Goleman.

Just a Call Away Series

This series is designed for customer service representatives whose basic responsibility is working with customers over the phone. The scenarios also are helpful for face-to-face contact, and discussions easily can be geared to either phone or direct customer contact.

The Really Angry Customer

This film demonstrates how to calm an angry customer, get the information you need to move to the next step, and avoid taking angry comments personally. Also included are practical tips for dealing with angry customers and for resolving problems and concerns in a helpful manner.

Attitude Is Everything

This film presents the concept of positive body language. It also covers intonations and other approaches necessary for delivering good service to each customer—on the phone and in person. Scenes show typical behaviors that can be turned around to provide the customer with a feeling of receptivity and concern.

It's Your Call

This film's scenario includes an older client with special needs, and highlights the essentials for achieving ever-increasing sales targets without jeopardizing good customer care. This is a good training tool for demonstrating effective cross-selling.

The Outbound Call

This film prepares representatives to make the most of each call by using skillful questioning to help close the sale. Provides examples of how to deal with rejection and how to get the support of the "gatekeeper."

Customers with a Difference

This film examines how to work with people whose first language is not English. Points out how stereotypes can hinder communication and shows how to overcome assumptions, speak clearly, give appropriate directions, and put the customer at ease.

Remember Me

One of the most widely used films in customer service training, this video follows a customer through several examples of unsatisfactory service, with lessons to be learned from each scenario. Shows how neglect and lack of basic respect create dissatisfied customers who will tell others about their experiences. It is useful in any customer service initiative.

Cliff's Customer Service Adventure

This fun training program is ideal for showing young frontline employees how to give responsible, caring customer service.

Attitude Virus: Curing Negativity

This is not specifically a customer service film, but it can be used as part of a discussion of the importance of attitude in serving customers, especially in stressful situations.

Call of the Mummy

Uses a unique approach to call-based customer service to demonstrate how a monotone voice and unsympathetic attitude can greatly reduce customer satisfaction.

Invisible Man Meets the Mummy

This fast-paced presentation shows that treating your customers as if they were invisible can lead to dire consequences.

It's a Dog's World

Made for healthcare trainers, this film uses humor to show that patient satisfaction is central to an organization's survival.

Communication in Healthcare

This film emphasizes the power of words and positive language when caring for the health of others.

Maxine Kamin is the founder and president of TOUCH Consulting, Inc.: **T**raining for **O**rganizational Development, **U**nparalleled Customer Service, **C**ommunications, and **H**uman Resources, headquartered in Plantation, Florida (www.touchconsulting.com). She has been avidly involved in leadership and customer service research and training for more than 25 years, and is the author of many publications, including *Uncommon Courtesy,* a training program that is enhancing customer service in 36 states.

Kamin consults with corporations, state and local governments, and nonprofit agencies to help individuals and teams reach their goals and attain success in the global marketplace. She formerly served as a faculty member at the University of Massachusetts, as acting dean at Miami-Dade Community College, and as manager of instruction and evaluation at American Express. She has trained thousands of associates, from corporate executives to frontline staff, and has received numerous awards and commendations for her personable and enthusiastic approach to training and consulting.

Kamin's company operates on the premise that the personal touch in business—respecting and appreciating associates and customers—is the key to success. Her programs are designed to give practical application to these principles.